One of the most (if not the most) valuable assets a person can have is relationship capital. Only a few understand this, practice it on a daily basis, and use it to build their success. Zvi is definitely one of them. His book draws on real stories and provides cogent advice, suggesting concrete steps readers can take to build their CAPITAL.

—ITZIK AMIEL
author of *The Attention Switch*

Zvi and Contactually have devised a clear process for helping pros keep their most valuable relationships strong, in a way that I have not seen before.

—DORIE CLARK
bestselling author of
Stand Out, Entrepreneurial You,
and *Reinventing You*

Zvi and his team have built a proven approach to growing your relationship-driven business and dominating the market—and he's giving it to you in this book!

—TOM FERRY
host of *The Tom Ferry Show* and
author of *Life! By Design*

SUCCESS
is in your
SPHERE

SUCCESS
is in your
SPHERE

Leverage the Power of
Relationships to **Achieve**
Your Business Goals

ZVI BAND

New York Chicago San Francisco Athens London Madrid
Mexico City Milan New Delhi Singapore Sydney Toronto

1 2 3 4 5 6 7 8 9   LCR   24 23 22 21 20 19

ISBN: 978-1-260-45283-9
MHID: 1-260-45283-2

e-ISBN: 978-1-260-45284-6
e-MHID: 1-260-45284-0

Library of Congress Cataloging-in-Publication Data

Names: Band, Zvi, author.
Title: Success is in your sphere : leverage the power of relationships to
   achieve your business goals / Zvi Band.
Description: 1 Edition. | New York : McGraw-Hill Education, 2019.
Identifiers: LCCN 2018060938| ISBN 9781260452839 (hardback) | ISBN
   1260452832
Subjects: LCSH: Career development. | Interpersonal relations. | Social
   networks. | BISAC: BUSINESS & ECONOMICS / Skills.
Classification: LCC HF5381 .B266 2019 | DDC 650.1/3--dc23
LC record available at https://lccn.loc.gov/2018060938

McGraw- Hill Education books are available at special quantity discounts to use as premiums and sales promotions or for use in corporate training programs. To contact a representative, please visit the Contact Us pages at www.mhprofessional.com.

For my father, who counted the stars—

and for his grandchildren,

may they likewise follow their purposes

CONTENTS

INTRODUCTION:
RELATIONSHIPS ARE OUR
MOST IMPORTANT ASSET

OK, let's get this out of the way. It's pronounced Z'vee. It should be pronounced Tsvi as it's spelled in Hebrew, but my parents decided to give me the really sweet Z as a first letter. (Yes, the name is Israeli. I was born in Boston.)

I'm an introvert. There's a high likelihood you are, too, given what we've learned about relationship-driven professionals. I'm such an extreme introvert that during my freshman year of university, I seriously considered going back to my parents' home every weekend just to avoid talking to people (don't cry for me, I ended up having a ton of fun for four years).

This tendency persisted when I started working for a large consulting firm. Our managers were always coaxing us to "new hire networking events" and telling us about all the opportunities to "connect" with others. I never believed that *networking* was an important career skill. In my mind, a room full of professionals trying to meet each other held the same promise of fear and awkwardness as the first slow dance at a friend's party. So I clung to the sidelines with people I knew.

My first day at the firm psychologically felt like nails on a chalkboard. And not in a "Hi, I'm the new hire, please tell me where the bathroom is" kind of way, but in a "I don't think this is what I'm supposed to be doing with my life" way. I had always had an interest in entrepreneurship, not because I had created dozens of businesses since I was a toddler, slinging candy bars in middle school for a 25-cent margin—I never did any of that. The best gift my parents gave me was to teach me to pursue my passion at all costs, for better or worse. As I learned on my first day on the job, that was not going to come from leading a development team at a government contractor. Something didn't fit. I saw everyone comfortably settling into their new roles, their careers, their work-life balance, but I was feeling anything other than comfortable. As the months went by, the value of pursuing my passion, instilled by my parents, kept directing me toward a more entrepreneurial route.

I realized that my desired path wasn't something I could simply apply for. I knew that meeting entrepreneurs or those with the same shared passion was important. So summoning confidence I didn't even know I had, I tossed myself into networking events, meetups, tweetups, and BarCamps—as many as three a week. If there were people there who might be interesting, I went. When I wasn't at work or trying to network in person, I tried to stay connected leveraging social media, then primarily populated by geeks and other early adopters.

Peter and I met at a small technology conference in DC. It took an incredible amount of effort to get me to step into that room that day in 2007 and introduce myself to people. He was one of the few I managed to connect with, enough to schedule a follow-up coffee meeting. Neither of us was proactive about nurturing the relationship, but as the local technology community was small and social media in its infancy, it was easy to keep tabs on each other.

Up until then, I was on the traditional career path: I could inch up the corporate ladder, buy a car, get a mortgage, raise a family, and pretend to care about sports on the weekend. But I couldn't do it. So I left the safe world of government contracting to scratch a growing itch, and I joined a small design agency as chief technology officer (CTO). However, not long after, deeply unhappy with the uncomfortable working situation, I abruptly quit, with no other job lined up. No job, no savings. There were other serious considerations: my father's cancer had returned, and he was scheduled for major surgery the next morning—from which he would never fully recover. That day was December 1, 2008. For those of you who don't get horrid flashbacks at the mention of 2008, that was the very day the federal government declared the United States was in a recession, which was the worst economic downturn since the Great Depression of the 1930s.

A few days later, I called Peter.

It wasn't out of desperation, nor was there an ask. I simply wanted to let him know I had left my employer and was looking for what to do next. Like the dozen or so other calls I made that day, it could have started and ended there.

Thankfully, Peter had a project he needed help with. And another few he could see down the pipeline.

Suddenly, I had a client! The world was, in just one phone call, suddenly less bleak. He and I ended up doing dozens of projects together.

But then my former employer decided he wasn't so wild about that idea, and threatened to make things very messy for Peter's business if I were to continue working with him. Peter sided with me and stood his ground—when he could just as easily have gone the other way—which saved me.

He introduced me to someone he knew, who had just closed a round of funding and needed a CTO. That was one of my biggest contracts.

I needed somewhere to work downtown. Peter gave me a desk.

This story isn't meant to hero worship Peter. Peter isn't a saint, nor was I a charity case. We weren't particularly close personally, and yet Peter hired me to work with him, went to bat for me, helped me find work space, and made introductions to people who would also become clients. He did all this without an interview process, long conversations, or any distrust. He knew and respected me, and I him.

Why?

You work with people you know. You help people you know.

Completely unintentionally and without realizing it, I had stumbled onto one of the most important truths about the professional world.

Without the relationships I had back then—knowing who I knew, or more important, *having them know me*—I would have been an unemployed software developer who likely would have returned to the golden handcuffs of a stable consulting job, never to venture out again.

Without the right relationships, I would not have become CTO of an enterprise software company, built a team, built a product, and been part of an acquisition soon after.

Without the right relationships, I would not have gone on to build a thriving boutique software development firm and to work with big industry names on challenging technical projects.

Without the right relationships, I would never have been able to start and grow Contactually, investors wouldn't have decided to invest, and we wouldn't have made the right hires for the business. Experienced mentors and advisors were made available to us solely because of mutual connections. Among others, I was introduced to Patrick Ewers, one of the top coaches for relationship marketing, whose theories deeply influenced our work and served as a foundation for the strategies you're about to learn.

And without the right relationships, this book never would have seen the light of day.

If there is one thing I've learned, it is this:

Relationships are our most important asset.

The best businesses and careers in the world are built on personal, authentic relationships. My early career experience gifted me with this knowledge, but it was still difficult for me to foster relationships. While I was able to grow that nascent software consulting business into a force that worked with household names that most freelancers would chop off a big toe to land, actively maintaining touch with the right people was a continuous challenge. I would meet people for coffee, and within a week, I would have completely forgotten about any opportunities, follow-ups, or personal details— sometimes even their names! Client projects would roll off, and I would be so overwhelmed with my current work that I would never reengage with them—although anyone will tell you that a critical part of business development in consulting is to maintain touch with past clients for repeat and referral opportunities.

Our reliance on relationship capital—the goodwill and reputation amassed between two individuals—in the human experience is well known and understood, but that doesn't mean it's not really hard. And if it was hard for me, I was certain it was hard for others like me.

While technology has enabled us to be more "connected" than ever, helping us understand, analyze, and improve our ability to engage with those we desire to, the negative ramifications are something we are only starting to fully wrap our heads around. Depression. Feeling *more* disconnected. Fewer people in our circle of trust. Taking a prescriptive and intentional approach to maintaining our key connections has never been more necessary.

I wanted to fix that. On May 15, 2011, I articulated my idea behind Contactually in a note-taking app. I wanted to build software that could help build and maintain relationships, in the face of the challenges the modern world puts in front of us that prevents us from presenting our personal, authentic selves.

The core problem our typical customer faces is how to prevent key relationships from slipping through the cracks. You may meet for coffee, but never talk again. You keep feeling that you should reach out to that person, but you don't know what to say. You forget people. People forget you. You'll walk out of a networking event, having spent $20 on admission and another $30 on weak drinks, to yield a stack of business cards and LinkedIn connections you'll never engage with.

We solve that through relationship marketing software that helps people track and maintain key relationships. But telling people how to click around a site serves no purpose if they don't know what they should be doing. Telling them who to engage with daily is fruitless if they don't have a clear idea of how to add value.

Software can help, but you need something more. You need a strategy. Seeding, nurturing, and profiting from relationships requires a strategy. Strategies take intention, goals, and planning to execute. Strategies take routine and habit to carry out. Strategies have desired outcomes. Strategy is powered by the right people, the right processes and actions, and the right tools. Relying on software alone is a nonstarter.

Relationship building is not rocket science. Doing it consistently over days, months, and years is the real challenge.

That's the idea behind relationship marketing. Building and maintaining relationships with key contacts is an implementable marketing strategy that can yield new, repeat, and referral business. If taken seriously and not done ad hoc, it can be optimized to simple rituals using the right tools.

WHO YOU ARE, AND WHY YOU ARE HERE

You care about professional relationships, the kind that will result in a more successful business, a better career, a bigger bank account.

These could be relationships whose primary purpose is transactional (you seek to eventually close one or more deals with them), beneficial to your current role (current clients, referral sources, vendors), or as a lifelong member of your professional identity. What matters is that there is a clear benefit to being associated with these individuals.

There are many different approaches, intentions, and methods. You could be a giver, for giving's sake. You could be a connector, where your success lies in connecting people. Maybe you are all about surrounding yourself with a community of like-minded people to help propel yourself forward. We'll flesh out the different goals in this book.

Relationships not only help unlock earning potential, they make you feel good at the same time. But let's be clear about our primary driver: we know that a core reason to care about and foster strong professional relationships is to propel our business and our career forward. We should be honest about that. But nurturing authentic relationships for personal satisfaction and doing so for professional gain are not mutually exclusive properties. They do not have to be in conflict. You can do both simultaneously. We'll show you how.

WHAT THIS BOOK IS

This book presents a framework and a process for building—and profiting from—strong, authentic professional relationships.

This is not a book on selling or closing deals. It is not a book on networking or how to work a room. Nor does this book claim to be the sole source of relationship marketing canon. You are not meant to follow it dogmatically. Rather, treat what you find here as a recipe with all the necessary ingredients, with you as the chef of your own strategy.

Most of what we know is the result of working with tens of thousands of businesses, and it is distilled here for you. You'll encounter a number of other expert voices throughout these pages. We've intentionally not sought out celebrities or people at the peak of their success. Instead, we've featured professionals on the front lines every day who have mastered various aspects of relationship marketing in their daily practice.

HOW TO USE THIS BOOK

Chapters 1 and 2 serve as the foundation for the book: why and how relationships are important in a professional context, and the extrinsic and intrinsic barriers to maintaining them. It's important to understand the whys of relationship marketing, so there's a fair bit of scientific research woven throughout these two chapters. If you are simply too eager to get going and want to jump to the tactics, I'll understand, just *believe* that science has proven that professional relationships are a key yet fading asset, and humans aren't naturally predisposed to be good at maintaining them, especially given how technology isn't exactly rewiring us for the better.

Chapter 3 is about understanding and setting your goals. Don't skip over this, as unfocused efforts and lack of direction lead to burnout and failure. Knowing exactly what you need to achieve from your sphere will serve as a guiding point around which to align all of your efforts.

In Chapter 4, I introduce the CAPITAL strategy, the real meat (or tofu, if you're vegan) of the book. Our strategy.

The remaining chapters are dedicated to detailing each component of the CAPITAL strategy. I include Key Takeaways for each chapter, as well as sections on tactics, aptly named Getting Tactical. And to make sure that you don't put the book down without doing *something*, I have a single Quick Win task you can accomplish right then, making you feel just productive enough to reach for that extra scoop of ice cream.

I would encourage you to follow the structure and order that we've laid out. That said, this is not a whodunit novel, in which reading the ending will completely spoil it for you (he was dead the whole time!). Depending on the strength of your own skill set, you may choose to focus deeply on some chapters and flip through others.

Use the components of the framework to construct a process of your own. Even if you decide to follow what we've developed as is, I beg you to constantly analyze it to ensure that it is appropriate for you, and to tweak it as needed.

There are a lot of other people who are much more intelligent than I who have offered valuable insight into relationship marketing, and the Reading List in Appendix D lists their work.

I set out to write this book because I've seen the dearth of available tactical and strategic thinking on this subject, and I want to help as many professionals as possible. If you simply do *one* beneficial thing that you wouldn't have done otherwise as a result of reading this book, writing it will have been worth it.

Great relationships grow great businesses. I am so excited to see where this takes you.

Let's get started!

PEOPLE DO BUSINESS WITH PEOPLE THEY KNOW

Nancy is a Realtor who focuses primarily on single family homes in the swanky northwest area of DC. She's watched the city's real estate market soar, as gentrification turned decaying brownstones into luxury condos and aging neighborhoods into "the next hot community" with more spinning studios and salad bars than you can count. She's established herself as the expert on many of these neighborhoods and is proud to have helped hundreds of families over the years "find a home" and make smart purchasing decisions. For someone who had to develop her business by cold-calling, she's built up enough of a network that she no longer feels a need to send out mailings to her target neighborhoods. Her reputation, by now, is golden.

Nancy is still active in the community. That's why she's spending yet another Saturday afternoon at another neighborhood barbecue on the lookout for past clients, business owners, or other acquaintances.

Out of the corner of her eye, she spots a familiar face, one she hasn't seen in years. It's one of her old clients, who bought his first condo eight years prior with her help. That property must have increased in value by 50 percent since he bought it—not bad! As she walks over to say hi, she notices he's pushing a stroller. And not just a single-seat stroller, but one of those double-wide strollers that barely fits on a DC sidewalk, never mind in a small condo. She reintroduces herself, and he starts acting uncomfortable. She asks how his apartment is working out for him. He sheepishly shares that he moved to a townhouse in another area two years ago.

Nancy maintains her smile and wraps up the conversation with small talk, but in her mind, it's over. She lost. He worked with another agent. She's suddenly overcome with a fear of failure, of never having another client again. She unlocks her phone and looks up average recent transactions in that neighborhood. Whenever she sees a house price, she quickly calculates what her expected commission would be. She knows she's doing fine for herself, but she can't help but think about how much his commission would have been—how many car payments.

There's also a sense of betrayal. It's like being in middle school again and finding out that two of your friends had a sleepover without you. She did such a great job shepherding him into his home. Why didn't he call her?

We've all been there.

You're flipping through your newsfeeds and you see that your neighbor just listed his house . . . with someone else.

One of your past coworkers just hired another firm to do the same kind of work you've been doing for years.

They should have worked with you.

That feeling of betrayal. Were you not good enough? Did you do something to insult them? How did you blow it?

As your mind quickly goes through anger, sadness, failure, introspection, and then back to sadness, there is one very clear signal that comes through.

You should have stayed in touch.

What would have happened if you had kept up the relationship? And how easy would it have been to do?

It's an unavoidable question that evokes endless self-recrimination, especially when we connect the dots and realize it's not an isolated incident. Countless opportunities have slipped

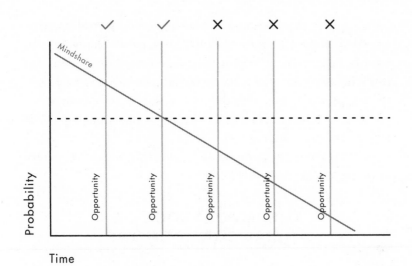

Opportunities fall through the cracks when relationships are not maintained.

through the cracks because the people tied to them have slipped away as well.

You are not alone. I have experienced this far too many times, as have hundreds of millions of other professionals.

I once met the CEO of what would come to be one of the largest and fastest growing companies of all time, when it was composed of 10 people. We have many mutual connections. What if I had stayed in touch?

This isn't just a feeling of a few emotionally insecure professionals. According to the National Association of Realtors, 88 percent of buyers say they'd work with their agent again. But in reality, only 12 percent of buyers work with the same agent again.

Something is broken.

You may have picked up this book in part because you feel the pain of relationships gone cold. I want you to know there is no shame in lost relationships, so you can prepare for the real work and discipline of counteracting the forces working to dissolve them.

I want you to understand the problem because I had to understand it for myself. I was faced with the exact same challenges you are when it came to managing my relationships. In order to treat the issue of fading relationships properly, we have to be aware of the symptoms and dig into the root causes. At the center of our problem, luckily, is not that we're bad professionals, or forgetful, or lazy. It's that we're human.

If there is one key takeaway I want you to have, it's this: *People do business with people they know.*

THE IMPORTANCE OF SOCIAL CONNECTIONS

Humans rely on social connections to help us filter out the subset of other humans we don't feel safe working with. We use personal interactions, secondary social proof, or the wisdom of the crowd to narrow down our options even further to the people we want to work with.

Most principles of relationship marketing are informed by neurology, psychology, and social science. Understanding the science helps frame the problem. Once you do that, you can create the strategy to fix it.

I shouldn't have to convince you of the fact that we are social creatures, and we rely on our social networks for business. You paid money for this book (you did pay, didn't you, good citizen?) because there was some trust that this would be worth your time. Maybe you know me. Maybe you work with my company and have faith that we know what we're talking about. Maybe a colleague or acquaintance recommended this book. Or maybe you read an online review and saw enough good ratings to convince you to check it out versus the latest book club pick.

There's a significant body of research on *social proof,* the reliance on what a trusted (or other) third party says about something that influences your decision.

Morton Deutsch and Harold B. Gerard were two of the earliest social psychologists to explore social proof in 1955. They

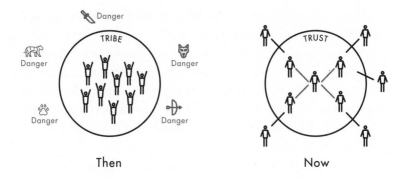

We are social creatures.

conducted an experiment in which participants were placed in groups. Participants were tasked with matching an image on one card with one of three on another, sometimes by memory. Deutsch and Gerard provided unanimously false answers to see how the participants were influenced.

They found participants were more susceptible to social proof during the memory test when they were more likely to experience uncertainty about their judgment. This was a key finding: *where there's uncertainty or absence of knowledge, there's an opportunity to influence.*

This social influence has not only been observed in natural behavior, but also in brain activity. Psychologists and physiologists alike have found adjusting to the majority is "reinforced via reward responses," whereas disagreement with the majority results in cognitive dissonance or even punishment responses.[1] Even if you have conviction in an idea, the presence of a conflicting idea held by the majority will trigger a sense of discomfort, which can only be remedied by conformity. That means that even if you have doubts about a person or a product, approval by others in your sphere of influence can sway your opinion.

We are also programmed to avoid strangers. From early childhood, the majority of us are told not to trust strangers. Don't look at them, don't talk to them, and definitely don't go anywhere with them. Even as we grow into adults with better judgment, we're reluctant to trust people we don't already know. And our parents' warnings aren't the only reason for this.

Trust is founded on common ground. This tendency to gravitate toward people with similar interests or beliefs is called homophily.[2] Whom would you trust more: someone who shares your beliefs and interests, or someone who opposes them? That's not to say it's impossible to trust someone who thinks differently from you, but it's not as easy.

"When individuals hold a variety of prominent values in common, they often tend to develop a sense of familiarity that renders the behavior of the other more predictable and, in turn, promotes trust."[3]

As Western society continues moving toward individualism, specialization, and more niche communities that cater to specific beliefs and values, it's becoming less desirable to interact with strangers.

The more we align ourselves with groups that mirror our specific interests and values, the less we feel compelled to trust people who don't share them. Without common ground, a relationship cannot be fostered.[4] It's not just about ensuring that prospects find you; it's about choosing who you want to work with!

It should come as no surprise that when I started my consulting business, I was eager to work with anyone who would look at me. I was on Craigslist, message boards, Facebook; I responded to anything and everything. Initially, I was grinding through $300 website builds and helping architecture firms get set up with Gmail. I remembered a line from a mentor early in my career: *Your business is formed just as much by who you choose not to work with as who you do choose to work with.*

As I moved from "putting food on the table" mode into a growth mindset, I took that to heart. I became more critical of any inbound requests. Yes, it was money, but would I want to work with this potential client? Is this a project I would be proud of?

Don't get me wrong—there were a ton of sites and applications we built because it was quick money. But I learned that the best projects were the ones that came from previous clients with whom I had a good groove or prospects who had been referred by a trusted third party. For years I had the standard "Contact Us" form on our site, but I rarely responded to those queries.

I wasn't afraid to do my due diligence and ask for references before working with a client. Crazy, right? Not really. If you are to form a partnership, there needs to be trust and respect both ways.

DEREK COBURN, WEALTH MANAGER AND COFOUNDER OF CADRE

As if running one of the top wealth management firms wasn't enough, Derek Coburn, alongside his wife, founded CADRE, an invite-only community of business professionals. CADRE is an antithetical response to mainstream transaction-minded networking events, at which everyone swaps business cards purely to chase that next opportunity.

My best friend is somebody who was a client first. A lot of my really good friends were clients of mine in my wealth management business or members of CADRE first, and I've never once felt any sort of ickiness or weirdness about our friendship as a result of that. I think that 95 percent of problems in business come from business owners making bad decisions on the front end about who we're going to work with. One of the ancillary benefits of having two businesses side by side is that I stick to my guns in terms of who is an ideal client. I've been able to expand that definition to include people who I really get along well with, people who fully buy into the value proposition that I'm offering.

I like the term passion prospecting. If I like drinking good wine and I host wine events on a regular basis for my clients and prospective clients, I'm going to attract people who have that in common with me, same with golf. That's part of it.

Whether you realize it or not, there's an intangible aspect of your business's clientele being, "I like working with this person. We have things in common."

It gets trickier coming at it from the other angle. In seeking out friends as potential clients, we have to have the desire to be extra diligent in making sure that it's going to be a good fit because coming at it from a friend-first perspective and then potentially having them be a client, you can ruin a friendship. Whereas a lot of my friends who became clients first, that wasn't a consideration in deciding if I was going to work with them or not.

We like to work with people we know, like, and trust. It sounds like common sense, but the reason for this can be found in *social capital* theory.

It's easiest to think of social capital as a collection of relationships and shared values that allow us to trust one another. And it's this trust and sense of commonality that make it so much easier to work together.

The late sociologist James Coleman demonstrated this idea by examining the tight-knit wholesale diamond market in New York City. While negotiating a sale, a merchant often passes a bag of stones to another merchant for inspection. There is no concrete insurance the inspecting merchant won't steal the stones and replace them with fakes. But since the market is connected by family, religious, and community ties, there is a sense of trust between the merchants that replaces "elaborate and expensive bonding and insurance devices," which, if in place, would impede the efficiency of the market's transactions.[5]

The key takeaway: once trust is established among two or more professionals, transactions become faster and easier, as there is reduced fear of any illicit or unfair activities.

TRUST LEADS TO SAFETY

It's hard to believe, but according to a study by the National Association of Realtors, in 2016, 5 percent of Realtors were victims of crime (e.g., identity theft, robbery, assault) perpetrated by their clients, and 39 percent experienced a situation that made them fear for their personal safety or the safety of their personal information.[6]

Trust is one of the most important factors in any working relationship. If we don't trust the people we're working with, there is little else that matters.

Beyond trust and safety, there is an economic driver behind the preference for working with people we already know. Your existing relationships can be the most cost-effective source of business. This exchange from *The Office* illustrates my point:

> RYAN: Is it cheaper to sign a new customer? Or to keep an existing customer?
>
> DWIGHT: Keep an existing . . .
>
> MICHAEL: Shut, it. . . . Uh, it's equal.
>
> RYAN: It is ten times more expensive to sign a new customer.
>
> MICHAEL: OK. Yes! It was a trick question.
>
> DWIGHT: Yeah, but look, I mean, he didn't need business school. OK, Michael comes from the school of hard knocks.[7]

Was Ryan making it up?

It's said that acquiring a new customer costs five times more than retaining an old one. Although this figure is often debated, the main idea remains: firms should spend more time and money on customer retention.

Return customers can be a gold mine if you keep them around. Business strategist Fred Reichheld stresses their strong potential:

> Return customers tend to buy more from a company over time. As they do, your operating costs to serve them decline. What's more, return customers refer others to your company. And they'll often pay a premium to continue to do business with you rather than switch to a competitor with whom they're not familiar.[8]

Of course, every customer starts as an acquisition, and there is no better channel to acquire new customers than through a referral program. Referrals provide higher contribution margins, greater retention, and overall better customer value.

In 2006, the American Marketing Association conducted an observational study spanning 33 months that looked at customers of a German bank. The study compared the current value of contribution margins and expected value six years after acquisition between referrals and nonreferrals.

After the observation period, it found referred customers had a 25 percent higher contribution margin than nonreferred customers. Referred customers were also 18 percent less likely to defect than nonreferred and were 35 percent more valuable!

Since customers often refer their friends and family, referred customers are likely to have greater trust and a stronger emotional bond with the company. They're also more likely to have discussed the company's features with the person who referred them. As a result, there's a greater chance they'll use its products or services more extensively than a nonreferred customer.[9]

Reputation Matters

Not only are we social creatures, but we are social creatures who use the reputations of the people around us to determine whether we will work with them.

Let's rewind a little bit, before Al Gore ever woke up one morning and "invented" the Internet. Say you were thinking about buying a house. You'd likely find a local agent, the thought never having crossed your mind to do much more than peruse the newspaper for the open houses listed for that weekend.

How things have changed.

Our parents' and our grandparents' generations could rest much easier than we can in the present day. What set them apart and made them stand out enough to be selected from a pool of professionals were three things: I'll refer to them as the *knowledge advantage*, the *skills advantage*, and the *reputation advantage*. Two of them are pretty close to dead today.

Having a *knowledge advantage* over many of your peers is a clear competitive advantage. Or, rather, it was. See, at some point, the education you paid for was necessary to gain the information required to perform the tasks expected of you. Your education, licensing, and/or capital also gave you access to exclusive resources. Doctors were the sole source of healthcare information and had exclusive resources to look it up. Real estate agents were the only way to get lists of homes for sale. Day trading wasn't a possibility except for a select few who could buy real-time stock feeds; the rest of us could only look at stocks when they were printed in the paper the next morning!

Now, we have WebMD, which allows us to walk into the doctor's office thinking we know more than the doctor does about our particular condition. Wikipedia, Zillow, YouTube, Khan Academy—these are just a few of the seemingly infinite fonts of free or low-cost information presently available. Since information is no longer a protected resource to be accessed by an elite few, the *knowledge advantage* is quickly decreasing in importance.

While greater access to information has caused disruption for business owners who used to be confident in their exclusive bank of knowledge, things are peachy keen because we have the *skills advantage* over others, right? Because your geographic location used to be all-important, you would work with the one or two professionals in your area. If you wanted to hire a plumber, you would open the *Yellow Pages* and pick a plumber from the few who served your area.

On second thought, in an increasingly connected society full of easy communication and collaboration tools and gig marketplaces, do we *really* need to be in the same city? If you can speak and see each other, edit documents, play games, even fly drones half a world away, the necessity of being collocated significantly diminishes. Take this book, for example. I'm based in DC, our publisher is in New York, our editors are in Houston and Denver, and the illustrator is in Kiev. Even local news can be written by people hundreds of miles away. Radiology reviews and surgical procedures can be directed from halfway around the world. If you think you can get by because you're the only one in your niche or area, think again.

That leaves one out of the three principles: the *reputation advantage*. While the other two have faded into irrelevance, having a great reputation is still key. Given our human hardwiring, this principle is likely not going anywhere.

To build a business, the right reputation matters.

If people do business with people they know, then we as business practitioners have to increase the number of people who know us. Sounds logical.

Not so fast. As Nancy saw in the opening of this chapter: just because people were in your sphere of influence *at some point* doesn't mean they will automatically keep you at the top of their list *indefinitely*.

There are forces working against us that are deeply ingrained in who we are. We are preprogrammed to trust and prefer to collaborate with those with whom we have a personal affiliation, but human psychology doesn't always make it easy.

KEY TAKEAWAYS

- People do business with people they know.

- Psychologically we're predisposed to trust people we believe are safe.

- People who know us are also the most cost-effective source of business.

- While knowledge and skills aren't effective competitive advantages today, our reputations still are.

2

THE BARRIERS TO MAINTAINING RELATIONSHIPS

Why do we fail to remember everyone we meet? Why is every happy past client not an automatic referral source? Why do people fail to follow up and stay in touch?

There are numerous forces working against us that prevent everyone from having the perfect sphere of influence. I'll walk you through them here so you understand how to counteract those forces when we lay out our strategy in later chapters.

While there are some relationship wunderkinds, the rest of us mere mortals have to rely on tools and rituals to give us an edge. I say edge because we know that most people won't put in the consistent work, will fail to regularly engage, or lack the discipline for the mundane tasks such as keeping notes of conversations. The people who do—hopefully you—have every opportunity to win. See it as an opportunity to distinguish yourself as the one who takes the structured approach and practices the routines. That alone can be one of your most powerful competitive advantages.

As we'll demonstrate later in the book, the strategies and tactics we propose aren't incredibly complicated—executing consistently is the real challenge. I want to reiterate that: the rituals and framework that we're going to talk about aren't rocket science; you will find the concepts pretty straightforward and simple. The complication, as we'll show in this chapter, is that a human (you) has to be involved in this.

BARRIER 1: WE CAN ONLY NATURALLY MANAGE SO MANY RELATIONSHIPS AT ONCE

Ugh, really?

Yep. There's been a great body of work to understand this, both from an individual psychological sense and from social dynamics. Here's a fun set of mental exercises for you:

- Name all of your old bosses going back to your very first job.

- How many of them would give you a reference?

- Name all the people who sat next to you in your office or cubicle, farm or dump truck. If they all called you today and asked for an introduction to one of your most valued relationships, how many of them would you do it for without hesitation?

- Who was at your wedding?

- If it was more than three years ago, how many of them would you invite again today?

- Flip through your connections on social networks. How many of them would you randomly text and invite for a drink, and how many would automatically say yes? If you were to ask them for $20, who would respond? What about if they asked you?

It was most likely a struggle to slog through that exercise, and I wouldn't be surprised if you stopped for an ice cream break a couple of times in an attempt to cheer yourself up. But, going back to

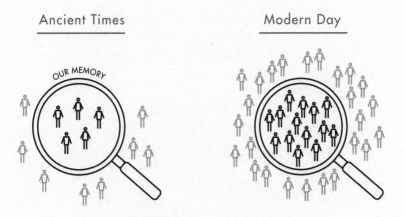

We can only manage so many relationships.

the research, it's not you. The number of people with whom we can have a relationship is naturally limited.

Although platforms like Facebook and Twitter allow us to amass thousands of friends and followers, the human brain is capable of keeping up with only a fraction of these relationships. Maybe that's why your ancestors had a paper Rolodex the size of a suitcase, and you don't know half the people in your phone?

Our capacity for relationships can be broken down into levels of intimacy. Our closest relationships, often with family, are limited to around five people. Relationships that are a step down in intimacy are limited to 15 of our dearest friends and family. The next 50 are more casual friends and extended family, and the next 150 straddle the fence between friend and acquaintance.[1]

Of course, these limits don't apply to every individual. Some can handle more relationships; some, fewer. We're not computers. According to sociologist and evolutionary psychologist Robin Dunbar, the average human only has enough mental capacity to keep up with a finite social network of 150 people, bar the more intimate relationships mentioned above. This is known as *Dunbar's number.* You hear Dunbar's number regurgitated repeatedly among "experts" on networking. What does it actually mean?

Dunbar tested this idea in 2001, when he looked at British households and how many Christmas cards they received in order to measure their social network size. The average network size among households was roughly 154, astonishingly close to his hypothesized 150.[2]

As for why our brains have a limited social network size, Dunbar theorizes it has to do with the size of our neocortex, the brain region most highly correlated with sociality. When studying apes, Dunbar found apes with larger neocortices had larger networks.[3]

Yes, there will be some outliers. I remember meeting one of them when I was in college; he was running an on-campus organization. As he was saying goodbye to 80 or so seniors, who had varied in their involvement, he was able to give off-the-cuff, incredibly detailed information about the past four years to each and every senior. The amount he was able to recall was stupendous—years later, I'm still impressed.

Some people can remember the most minute details from the most trivial events, like what their mother was wearing on April 5, 1989. While there is nothing special about that particular memory, for people with Highly Superior Autobiographical Memory (HSAM), it's readily available for retrieval. You probably grew up calling this photographic memory, but the ability to take precise mental snapshots of an image is little more than a myth.[4] That high school classmate who was boasting about possessing photographic memory? You finally have some ammunition against him at your thirtieth reunion.

The National Institutes of Health define HSAM as an "ability in which individuals are able to recall events from their personal past, including the days and dates on which they occurred, with very high accuracy."

The point: if you aren't the type of person who can easily maintain many hundreds of relationships and recall even the slightest details about people you've met, then technology, process, and discipline are necessary.

BARRIER 2: RELATIONSHIPS DECAY

How many people do you think you've met in your life? Hundreds? Thousands? Tens of thousands?

How many people are in your social circle right now? To sum it up, every relationship is on an escalator going down. Over time, without taking the steps to build that relationship up, we'll be back to the ground floor.

Imagine putting $20 under your mattress and coming back six months later to find you only had $15. Not an enjoyable experience. While money doesn't simply fade away, our memory does. With that, so do the goodwill and reputation that others have with us.

The slipping away of goodwill between two people, or what we call the *time decay of mindshare*, is a completely natural thing. It's part of the human condition.

PATRICK EWERS, FOUNDER AND CEO OF MINDMAVEN

In addition to being my coach and friend for years, Patrick Ewers also runs Mindmaven, an executive coaching organization focused on helping professionals reach their fullest potential through personal leverage and relationship marketing.

Ever sat down with someone for the first time in months only to hear, "I wish you'd reached out sooner! I had the perfect opportunity for you!" We've all been there, and it's easy to feel frustrated with the other person. But the truth is, we only have one person to blame: ourselves.

Why? Because our ability to generate referrals is largely driven by mindshare, or how top-of-mind we are, and mindshare is dynamic—driven largely by how we interact with our relationships.

Let me explain with an example: imagine you meet up with Mike for lunch. Immediately following that lunch, you're at 100 percent mindshare, meaning if he encounters a relevant opportunity, he's very likely to think of you. Good, right? The problem is, that doesn't last.

As days, weeks, and months pass without meaningful interactions, your mindshare begins to decay; and as it does, so does the likelihood Mike will think of you in the face of opportunity.

That's why when you meet up months later and he says, "You would've been perfect for this! I can't believe I didn't think of you," it's not his fault. The truth is, Mike's brain was physically incapable of thinking of you because you allowed it to be rewired to focus on more relevant relationships.

You dropped the ball, not him. The good news is, this is entirely avoidable. Mindshare is controlled by the quality and frequency of the interactions we deliver. Let me illustrate.

You have lunch with Mike, and your mindshare's at 100 percent. The next day, you send a follow-up e-mail expressing how much you enjoyed the interaction. A few weeks later, you send a blog post you think he'd find valuable, followed by an introduction a month later, then a meaningful birthday message a few weeks after that.

With interactions like that, your mindshare never decays below a certain threshold. As a result, the likelihood of Mike thinking of you in the face of relevant opportunities practically skyrockets. That's the power of mindshare, and why this book is dedicated to equipping you with powerful tactics to maintain it.

For the rest of us who don't have HSAM, we are prone to forget. There are a handful of widely accepted theories that explain why memory loss occurs. Some are time-based, while others are event-based.

Time decay theory suggests memories dull as time passes. The longer a memory is neglected, the harder it will be to retrieve. In fact, as soon as attention is "switched away" from a newly processed memory, it becomes harder to access. This is because the processing of new memories takes up the same "limited attentional resource." In other words, your brain processes new memories at the expense of maintaining old ones. However, if rehearsed, the memory will stick around longer.[5]

> *Every time I learn something new, a little of the old gets pushed out of my brain.*
> —HOMER SIMPSON[6]

The most common event-based memory loss theory is *interference*. It suggests that the encoding of new memories pushes older memories out. A more detailed model of interference, the Serial Order in a Box (SOB) model, suggests encoding strength is "novelty sensitive." Essentially, new memories are more likely to be encoded if they differ from older ones. Naturally, if they're too similar to older memories, they'll be harder to encode.[7]

Although there isn't a list of personality traits or behaviors that make an individual unforgettable, there are circumstances in which first impressions can strengthen memory retention.

Research has found that stress experienced "after acquiring information about a previously unknown person strengthens the memory of the newly formed impressions for positive personality traits."[8]

A study conducted in Germany exposed participants to a series of photos with accompanying personality traits. Some participants were subjected to stressors after seeing the faces, while others were a control. Those exposed to stressors after being exposed to the faces demonstrated better memory retention when later asked to identify the accompanying personality traits. More specifically, participants had the strongest memories of those photos associated with positive personality traits.[9]

Inducing stress after every coffee meeting to aid memory simply isn't workable, but this interesting piece of research helps us identify why we remember some interactions (first dates, interviews) over others.

Key takeaway: because our memory decays, we have to be intentional about the tools and processes we use to retain information relevant to our relationships.

BARRIER 3: OUR SOCIAL NETWORKS CHANGE AS WE AGE

As we get older, our social network size inevitably shrinks. Ask yourself, how many friends does your mother have? You can probably count them on your hands.

There are two theories that explain why our social networks change: *socioemotional selectivity theory* and *social convoy theory*.

True to its name, *socioemotional selectivity theory* describes how people change their network size based on their social and emotional needs. Think about a teenager who looks into the future and sees an unlimited amount of time ahead of her. She wants to make as many diverse connections as she can. Now think about her grandmother, who doesn't have as much time. She wants to interact with only the most important people in her network (family and intimate friends) who can fulfill her social and emotional needs.

Social convoy theory has less to do with how you feel and more to do with where you are in life. There are a handful of formative life events most of us go through that increase our social network. Transitions from elementary to secondary school to college, marriage, and job entry tend to increase our social networks because of the connections we make as we go through them. However, some events like transitioning into parenthood or losing a spouse and nonnormative events like losing a child or getting divorced decrease our network.

Of course, it's not one or the other. Looking at your life now, you probably notice it's a combination of both. The general trend

You, age 18   You, age 45

Our network size is related to where we are in life.

shows an increase in network size during adolescence and young adulthood, but a "continuous decrease" afterward.[10]

Your professional self, simply as a function of aging, will be less connected than you were as a teenager.

BARRIER 4: STRONG RELATIONSHIPS ARE GETTING MORE COMPLICATED THAN EVER

Internet = Volume

With our increasing ability and reliance on connection, our own limitations pose an even greater threat.

When we were hiring for a position in quality assurance and struggling to find the right fit locally, we shared the posting online—and we were approached by hundreds of people within a short period of time. We ended up hiring two great candidates in Ukraine after interviewing people from around the world. If you have ever posted a project opportunity on an online classifieds site or freelance matching service, you are well aware of the inundation of good candidates one receives—globally.

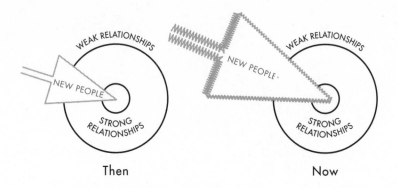

The Internet greatly increases our opportunities for new relationships.

Local networking isn't immune to the new challenges posed by the Internet either. While in the past you may have only needed to contact one or two professionals your neighbors recommended, now you may have any of the hundreds or thousands in your service area contact *you* via an increasing number of sources.

If, while searching for a real estate agent, you were to fill out a request on an online portal, click around on a local real estate brokerage website, e-mail the neighborhood listserv, and post on Facebook, it would be shocking if you had any less than two dozen qualified agents pinging you within a few hours.

JOHN CORCORAN, COFOUNDER OF RISE25

John Corcoran is one of the best connectors I know. He works with the full spectrum of entrepreneurs, from solo to Fortune 100, helping them turn relationships into revenue.

Fighting the Commodity Comparison

If you're in a commodity market, you need to move yourself out as much as possible so that people aren't making a direct apple-to-apple comparison between you and someone else. This happens a lot in law, as an example. It's very easy for lawyers to become a commodity, where people are just competing on price. The last thing you want to hear is, "Well, I talked to this one lawyer that you recommended, but he charged $3,000, while this other lawyer was $1,300. So we went with the $1,300." That's a commodity comparison. Lawyers who market for clients based on price eventually lose because it's a race to the bottom. You need to make enough of an argument to pull yourself out of the commodity comparison. To the extent that you can, with whatever it is you do, make it so that people aren't able to make a direct comparison between you and something else, or so it is very difficult to make that calculation. It's going to be much easier to get people to buy what you're selling.

If you as a consumer have hundreds of options at your fingertips not previously available, what does that say for the people who hire you? Or the people who have hired you or could refer you? They have even more options and are approached by more people every day. Staying buoyant in the current requires constant paddling.

BARRIER 5: WE'RE WIRED TO THINK IN THE SHORT TERM

If I were to offer you $5 today or $100 in a year, you would almost certainly choose $5 today. I know I would, mainly because the pastry display at the coffee shop where I'm writing is giving me a very welcoming look.

You're instinctively wired to prefer short-term gains to long-term benefits. If lightning struck and our priorities reversed to favor the long term, gyms would have lines out the door, and the world would have no idea what a milkshake was. Something that yields little to no immediate value is therefore much harder to execute consistently.

Say you're hungry, and you want some vanilla ice cream. You hit up the local diner and find out all that's left is chocolate. They won't be getting another shipment of vanilla for another three days. You order chocolate. Why? Because you're human. Rather than wait, you want an immediate reward, even if it's not as good as what you could have had by waiting.

This behavior is known as *hyperbolic discounting*, and you've probably fallen victim to it before.

"When humans are offered the choice between rewards available at different points in time, the relative values of the options are discounted according to their expected delays until delivery."[11]

That behavior plays a role here. When we are offered the choice between what gives us instant gratification now and what pays off months or years later, we tend to choose the first option. The best networks are the ones that yield tremendous value over a long period of time but may not deliver anything predictable on a short time horizon.

A past home buyer may not be ready to move for five to six years or more. A repeat business opportunity is uncertain. That person who is looking for some free advice for her young business—one could wait years before she is in a state to afford your services, if at all. That company you've been trying to network your way into may not have the right role for you for another year or two, and who says you're a fit for it? With all of these possibilities, we might understand the long-term opportunities available to us. But as we think about what we want to do in the moment, it's hard not to get sucked into the short term.

Do we suit up and head to the gym, or do we watch another episode of *30 Rock* for some laughs? Do we plow into that giant bowl of kale or microwave that Hot Pocket? Should we reach out to a few past clients or flip through our Facebook feed for a little hit of dopamine? Which option is more tempting to do right now?

I faced a related challenge. As a freelancer, I knew I wanted to leave my contract work to build and sell my own software product. I had every ability to work on it and could have dedicated as much as half of my week to that pursuit, making enough money to comfortably get by. But week after week, my product remained unbuilt.

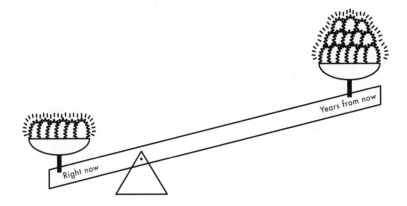

We need to balance short-term and long-term opportunities.

Why? Because as much as I wanted to create a product that could deliver long-term value, I was offered good money by clients who wanted their work done *now* and would pay me *now*. I was losing the fight over my time.

Our software system Contactually would never have been more than an entry in Evernote and a prototype had I not figured out how to tackle it. I was able to eke out some discipline in my schedule and devote time to building out product, and now, with my team, we've created a system that will provide immense value over the long term.

It's no different with our connections. We have to be in it for the long term with our relationships.

We'll talk in later chapters about strategies to overcome short-term mentality. It's just important to realize *it's how we're wired*.

Go back to that backyard barbecue at the beginning of Chapter 1, the moment when one of Nancy's former clients sheepishly admits that he worked with someone else, having completely forgotten about her.

Have you been there? Of course you have, and it's not the client's fault. Nor is it yours, so stop feeling deficient. Instead, let's work on a strategy to ensure that person is the last to ever forget you.

PERSPECTIVE #1: IMPORTANT VS. URGENT—WHAT WINS?

Picture yourself waking up in the morning, showering, having breakfast, walking your dog, and then commuting to the office. You grab a cup of coffee, sit down at your workstation, and pick up right where you left off at 5:01 p.m. the day before. You are simply working on the task at hand, plowing through the action items your job entails.

But then you're interrupted by a buzzing in your pocket with a notification from a random app, a pop-up on your screen with an urgent request from your supervisor via work chat, a phone call from a vendor, and a desk fly-by from an officemate. And then there's the lurking suspicion that somewhere in the cloud sits a list of messages from all over the world, which may or may not require instant action.

One of the biggest challenges that a modern-day information professional faces is the battle of important vs. urgent.

Important actions are the needle-movers for your business and your career, well thought out, planned, and prioritized.

Urgent actions are time-sensitive and often done in reaction to someone else.

In an ideal world, we would sit down at 9 a.m. with our cup of green tea and get to work on the highest leverage, most impactful tasks for our job and our company, doing just that until it was time to go home.

Remember the last time you did that? We don't either.

We all know that, regardless of intentions, urgent items always interrupt our important work.

A software engineer might be deep in code, trying to solve a major technical challenge that will be a breakthrough for the company (important). But he's interrupted by a frantic customer service representative, who is on the phone with a major customer having an issue (urgent).

A lawyer might be hammering down terms of a large contract (important) when an old client calls out of the blue, needing a quick response to a negotiation he's handling (urgent).

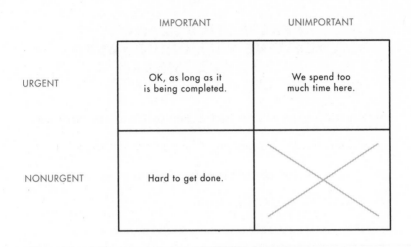

Urgent items can interrupt our important work.

In the modern era, our biggest professional folly is arguably the habitual acceptance of urgency over the prioritization of importance. The resulting focus on the near term and instant gratification further wears away at the time and space we are able to dedicate to longer-term objectives. As newer communications technology further decreases the friction between two people, the ease of interrupting and being interrupted grows exponentially. As I write this paragraph, I can safely assume there are two or three new e-mails waiting for me, one or two text messages, half a dozen notifications from various communication tools, and 200+ social posts from people whose opinion I suddenly decide to care about at 3 a.m.

This is proven. Seventy-one percent of people report being interrupted frequently in the workplace. Fifty-six percent of people say that when they get interrupted they frequently leave work feeling like they didn't accomplish much.[12]

It's too easy to become interruption-driven in our lives, responding to whatever is thrown at us. Repeat after me: my inbox is just a list of actions that other people want me to do.

Ensuring you delineate and balance the execution of important tasks versus your reaction to urgent requests is a critical component of the modern-day professional experience.

PERSPECTIVE #2: NOT EVERYONE WILL DRIVE VALUE TO YOUR BUSINESS

Imagine if every person you met said one of the following things:

- Getting my business would be worth $5,000 to you.

- I'm absolutely going to be buying a home in October.

- I have the perfect job for you.

- I will refer six clients to you over the next year.

- No, I am not going to work with you or refer any business to you. Don't waste your time with me.

OK, snap out of that daydream.

When we meet someone, there is no guarantee that contact will generate any business value, or that person will even be enjoyable to work with! It would be insane if we assumed that every lead coming in the door was a sure thing. Do we think that every client we have will need our services again? The truth is, there is no certainty. We have nothing but educated hunches regarding who will drive business value to us, who won't, and to what degree.

This can be completely unrelated to your actions. Some people are natural givers, always looking for opportunities to help. Some are takers, who may put little thought toward your needs. One might turn out to have a large web of strong connections, while another may have a smaller network of loose connections. Some business relationships may take off like a rocket ship, while others tread water for years.

Simultaneously, there are numerous people in my network who, on the surface, seem like they could be incredibly helpful with introductions. But time and time again, no matter how much value I provide, they come up dry when I make the ask.

Millions of dollars are invested into software products that can provide, at best, *a guess* as to which leads are more likely to buy. Lead scoring algorithms pull in tons of different data points and engagement metrics to see who *might* be worth prioritizing. We'll talk later about how to prioritize your network so you are able to balance your time among different groups of relationships and build your sphere of influence. However, we have to be comfortable with the idea that we're placing (educated) bets as to who may be helpful in the long run. And, just like the stock market or gambling in Vegas, it's about the portfolio strategy across many different bets.

KEY TAKEAWAYS

- While we rely on relationships to determine whom we work with, we're not hardwired to easily retain or reinvigorate these relationships.

- Just as our memory decays, so does the knowledge and goodwill between people.

- This truth is only accelerating in the Internet age, in which we have more people than ever to connect and work with—and we're not always sure who matters.

- Some relationships may take years to bear fruit, which poses a challenge when we're predisposed to short-term gains and urgent issues rather than long-term strategies and important opportunities.

CHAPTER

3

SETTING THE BASELINE: UNDERSTANDING YOUR GOALS

This might be the most important part of the book, so allow me to repeat two key, yet conflicting, points. This conflict is the primary driver of this tome.

- Building and maintaining great relationships provides a cost-effective and potentially infinite source of opportunities to propel your business, but it happens with varying frequency over long periods of time.

- Professionals, especially in the current "instant" era, struggle to prioritize long-term, important tasks.

The key to relationship marketing lies not necessarily in any one tactic. *It's in your ability to consistently execute over a long period of time.* That's it.

Seems simple, right? I implore you not to underestimate how challenging this is, and therefore how seriously you must attack the challenge of repetition. Entire industries thrive on this; do you think gyms would be able to handle all the members on auto-renew if even half of them showed up on a daily basis?

If you take this conflict—and the desire to overcome it—seriously, you'll invest in the relationship marketing people, process, and systems in order to consistently execute.

Resolutions are meaningless. Strategic plans win.

If we merely *aspire* to build our sphere of influence in spite of all of this resistance, we significantly reduce our chances of yielding a satisfactory outcome. But with a little bit of planning and preparation and a lot of consistent execution, we can overcome those hurdles. If we have a *plan*.

One of the most important aspects of our relationship marketing strategy—or any strategy, for that matter—is to have a crystal clear idea of your goal, your North Star. There are so many things we could be doing with our time, money, and resources that if we don't have a clear outcome in mind, something we hope to get out of our efforts, relationship marketing will feel like a waste of time.

> *The price of anything is the amount of life you exchange for it.*
> —HENRY DAVID THOREAU

To justify our investment of time, energy, and dedication, we must ask *what's in it for me?*

Now, because I'm a level-15 mind reader, I know that there's something lurking in the back of your mind.

THE "ICKY" FACTOR OF RELATIONSHIP MARKETING

Icky. What a terrible word when you think about it.

But it's an appropriate label for that feeling we may have as we're thinking through our relationship marketing goals, as we're talking about "getting" something out of our sphere of influence. You may have felt that, too. These are *people* after all—people we're supposed to genuinely care about, who care about us.

Am I using others?

Am I not being genuine with people if I really just want their business?

Am I a sleazeball?

You might be asking yourself these questions and thinking, how can I leverage my relationships to achieve my goals and *not* use people?

Keep in mind the underlying truth that relationship marketing is built on: *people do business with people they know.* You know that goes both ways, right? You want to do business with people you know.

We want to help you strategically build relationships with others so *they* will want to work with *you.* However, you want to ensure that you're working with the best people possible, too, right? In most professions in which we eat what we kill, it's just as important to work with the right customers as it is to get the business. Prior to starting my own consulting firm, I received the best piece of advice from a PR veteran: *your business is formed just as much by the people you don't work with as the people you do work with.*

When I started my consulting firm, I was fortunate enough to get to a point where I could choose what projects I took on. Beyond setting up project minimums, I realized that my best clients were the ones that *came to me via someone I knew.* So I stopped responding to inquiries via my contact form and instead prioritized any business opportunity that came via someone I knew. My website served little more purpose than an electronic business card.

When you're building and executing your strategy to stay in touch and add value to key relationships, it's *not* so you can squeeze another dollar out of them. It's so you can determine if you *want* to work with them. That's really important because with this in mind, you can set out with a focus on building deep, valuable connections. The woman you met at a networking event who seems totally uninterested? Not worth it. The investor who kept playing around on his phone the whole meeting? Don't bother. The business owner who has a track record of being "the nightmare client"? Is he worth your time on earth?

When you are approaching your network strategically, it's not about finding a new way to interrupt people's days and shoving your message in front of them so relentlessly that they capitulate and work with you. Remember, *you are the product* that they're buying. You want to bring as much energy into these relationships as you would with a friend or family member. Because you *do* want them to be just as close as a friend or family member. The systematic approach you're implementing is helping *you be you.* It's not replacing you. It's showing who you are.

Technology won't build the relationship for you, it can only aid it. It can help you figure out who to talk to, when to talk to them, and give you ideas on what to say or do. Ultimately, all it's doing is helping represent who *you* are. It's up to you to be the person that they want to have a connection with.

SHAY HATA, REALTOR

Shay Hata moved to Chicago in 2013 to pursue real estate full-time. She started out in a new city with no sphere of influence and no previous experience selling homes. She quickly rose to be one of the top referred agents not only because of her amazing client service but because she leveraged her background in marketing and technology.

What's cool about this business is that we're working with people in one of the most important, emotional transactions of their lives. They're at their most vulnerable, so it's natural for them to want to work with people who they truly feel they're friends with or become friends with during the process. It's natural for me, in turn, to be close with the people I work with. Of the 75 guests at my wedding, 50 of them were clients at one point. They come over for brunch; our kids have playdates. Why should there be a separation?

So should you feel uncomfortable with the idea that you're "using" people? No—you care about building your business around people that you believe are the best fit, that you have a genuine connection with. And all of the strategies in the following chapter are there to help you be the best you can be.

So to develop our relationship marketing strategy, we first have to . . .

START WITH WHY

The answer to why is an important first step in building relationships. We need to understand the core motivation guiding us. The why also forms the nucleus of our strategy. By clearly defining our core intent, we can branch out from there, comfortable that everything we do leads back to our core why. This is no different than having a mission statement for your business, a North Star under which everyone you work with aligns themselves.

What is the intended goal or goals of your relationships? These aren't mutually exclusive of each other.

Money. Don't be afraid to admit that money is an important goal for you. That is a primary motivator, and enables many other things (family, travel, independence, bringing back Crystal Pepsi).

Happiness. Being happy is what we often strive for every day. There are many other factors that affect our happiness: order, cleanliness, peace of mind, etc.

Social status. Human beings are social creatures. We aren't designed to be lone rangers. We may seek power and influence over others, or long to be appreciated or thought of in a certain way. For some, simply being known as the "connector" can be gratifying.

New opportunities. Sometimes we just want to be kept on our toes. Yes, it might be more practical, like a better job, but other times, we simply want to be challenged.

If you're finding yourself stuck, or with a seemingly shallow answer, a really good trick is to have someone ask you "Why?" Then answer—five times over. This simple exercise will often help you get to the root of what you want. For example, relationships are important to me because I want to hire great people. Why? Because I want Contactually to grow. Why? Because I want to build a great company. Why? Because I enjoy building. Why? Well, from an early age I've always loved building things, and have a passion for creation. So only four whys, but we can clearly see that what motivates me is building.

So I will ask you one more time: *Why do you want to build and maintain relationships?*

Once we've identified the ultimate goal—the why—behind our relationship marketing strategy, we can get to the how: how we can leverage a strong sphere of influence to achieve our ultimate objective, and how we determine which relationships are important to us. If we don't generate a clear idea of how we want other people to affect our desired outcome, we risk aimlessly wandering through a sea of irrelevant people, burning up all the time and work we have invested so far.

CONSIDER *HOW* RELATIONSHIPS WILL HELP YOU ACHIEVE YOUR ULTIMATE GOAL

Think about how your relationships can help you satisfy your why. I'll go into a few possible answers to this question, but this is one of the choose-your-own-adventure portions. You could argue all your relationships are essential, but it's helpful to rank them according to your needs.

Will Relationships Help You Close More Business?

You walk into a franchise of a global coffee chain. You go up to the counter and order a drink, pay, grab your coffee, and walk out the door. Most likely by the time you've passed the threshold, you've forgotten everything about the barista behind the counter.

Your line of business likely requires a little more of a relationship. It's a people business. Your clientele aren't buying just what you're selling, they're buying into your expertise, your skills, your advice. A lawyer isn't selling legal contracts, she is selling her time, years of expertise, and ability to guide a company through major decisions (otherwise everyone would just download a template off the Internet). A real estate agent isn't selling the house or even facilitating the transaction. Her value is her ability to wade through the sea of houses and potential buyers, be the trusted advisor through one of the biggest financial transactions of a family's life, and help her clients protect that monstrous asset.

Is Your Day Job a Commodity? How Many Others Can Provide the Same?

In Chapter 2, we discussed that *knowledge* and *skills* as competitive advantages are rapidly diminishing in our generation. We're at a point where access to knowledge is increasingly universal, so having the means to acquire that knowledge is no longer as much of a differentiator. This means that differentiating yourself becomes even more important, and the best way to do that is through your relationships.

For example, you can take a short course to learn the basics of real estate. Hundreds of online educational sites exist to teach us just about anything, from coding to financial modeling. As the world gets more and more connected, the sphere of potential service providers we have access to gets bigger and bigger. If we need firewall software, we don't have to go to the local IT shop. If we decide to buy a house, we're not going to just look at the nearest bus stop advertisement or postcard in the mail. Because of this, who we are becomes all the more important.

To some degree, the actual work that we do is table stakes. While we may be great at it, so are others. Since people aren't just looking past you at the product or service you're selling, who you are in their eyes matters all the more. People work with people they like, so in order to work with someone, it's important to be likable and, most important, to *remain* likable.

Your ability to build a deeper and more genuine relationship is your competitive advantage, differentiating yourself from others around you and allowing you to close more business faster.

How Important Is Retaining Existing Business?

Getting a customer is the lion's share of the work. If we can retain that customer at a lower cost than replacing that customer, why aren't we spending more time staying engaged with our existing customers?

We mustn't fool ourselves into thinking that we will gain a customer for life just by gaining that customer. As a specific industry example, according to the National Association of Realtors, 88 percent of homebuyers initially said that they would work with their agent again. But only 12 percent do.[1]

A large driver of our relationship marketing strategy is not just about *becoming* known. It's about *remaining* known.

Are Your Relationships a Primary Source of New Business?

We know that technology has lowered the barrier of entry for connecting people with professionals. We know that technology has widened and multiplied the possible communication channels through which we can share information with people we trust. We most likely rely on word-of-mouth or at least a community of people we trust to point us the right way.

Combine these two, and we're right back to one of the best paths of business generation: someone the buyer trusts. Whether via inbound referral or outbound introduction, the transitive nature of trust and relationships (Beth trusts Jack, Jack trusts me, therefore Beth trusts me) propels us into the trusted circle of people who someone would work with. For many lines of business, we can rely on the words of the masses (any directory site with online reviews), but for many, many more, it's still the point-to-point recommendations that raise us above the noise.

That requires having a network of people that, when the time comes, would serve as our ambassadors and scouts.

Do You Just Like to Network?

This is a tough one. We often are led to believe that networking, or having a network, is itself an asset. Yes, absolutely. We may in fact be driven by just being known to a lot of people, having a lot of friends, etc. But, again, why?

If it's not to better close business, generate new business, or retain existing business, people can still drive other opportunities to us. One of the common types of opportunities that people look to generate is new jobs. Hiring companies rely on people they trust to hire the best talent.

Before you say, "I just want to network," identify what it is that you truly seek to gain by having a network. The risk of not having a clear North Star is not being motivated enough to keep at it every day.

JAYSON GAIGNARD, FOUNDER OF MASTERMIND TALKS AND AUTHOR OF *MASTERMIND DINNERS*

One thing that stands out about Jayson Gaignard is how he has curated an incredible sphere of influence of enviable household names, all while being an insanely humble and giving person.

Are your relationships for the job you have today or for life?

For the most part, anybody that I invest time and resources in I see a long-term relationship with. It may benefit me now. But even if I didn't do what I'm doing now, five years from now I still want to be friends with them. A lot of my energy is allocated toward nurturing relationships with our existing client base and nurturing relationships with people who we think would be good potential clients. If our business were to evaporate tomorrow, I would start a new business where the same people would come into play.

Are You Building a Brand?

Sometimes we just want to make a name for ourselves or to be known or highly regarded among a target group of individuals in our industry. Wanting to improve your personal reputation is not mutually exclusive of anything else listed previously, but it necessitates different tactics. You need an even larger segment of people to think of you as a thought leader or influencer.

As with general networking, ensure that you have a desired goal in building your reputation. For example, one goal might be new business. When I was consulting, I spoke, taught, and blogged often, so cold inbound opportunities were not such strange occurrences.

What Is the Output of My Relationship Marketing?

We've been pretty heady in this chapter so far—by now I think you probably deserve a jog around the block. After that, let's keep pushing through. Developing that clear idea of what you are aiming to achieve out of your relationship marketing efforts is the foundation on top of which we will be able to execute a strategy.

We talked about the different purposes of our relationship marketing: closing business, generating new business opportunities, retaining existing business, maintaining differentiation. What are the outputs of those different threads? *What should I get from my relationships?*

BUSINESS GROWTH . . . MONEY

Life is short, so let's not dance around it. Money is the primary way we transfer, store, and measure value in the present age (as opposed to food, livestock, gold). It's natural then that a primary way to measure the value of our relationship marketing efforts is by the amount our business or career grows. Revenue is the indicator of a business. If a lead I follow up with buys from me, that's clear monetary ROI.

While the ultimate goal may be revenue growth—likely through more sales—the primary output that we're looking for from our sphere is not necessarily more closed business. Rather, we are looking for that which leads to more business opportunities. Call them leads, requests for proposals, introductions, job posts, what have you—it's up to you to close them, but up to your sphere to help you source them. Repeat after me: *my sphere is here to give me more opportunities.*

Referrals

It's important to identify that we may not gain direct value from a relationship, but rather something that leads to value. If I get a referral from someone, that referral doesn't store value. But that referral could turn into a customer, who is of great value.

Completion of a Key Objective

Another output could be a tangible result that contributes qualitatively to business growth.

I spend most of my time hiring. We get applications and hire from all sources. That said, our top recruits originate via referrals from our network. There's clear value in a good new hire.

To help you measure the ROI, throw a dollar value on what the product of a successful relationship is to you. In the case of recruiting, we pay $2,000 for an internal referral ($1,000 to you, $1,000 to a charity of your choosing), so we can say a good job candidate is worth $2,000.

TONY CAPPAERT, COFOUNDER AND COO OF CONTACTUALLY

I've mentioned before how Contactually itself would almost certainly not exist were it not for the right people showing up at the right time. I met Tony just as I was completing the prototype.

Looking back, I think my college experience very much emphasized skills and knowledge over networking and relationships. Early in my career, I took pride in what I knew, not who I knew. I wasn't investing enough in the people in my sphere.

That changed when I started to get more involved in the start-up community. The most effective founders and leaders I know are those who surround themselves with people who are smarter than they are. I've tried to emulate their success as we've built Contactually.

Relationships are critical to what I do. As cofounder and COO of a software start-up, I'm responsible for driving high growth, but candidly, I don't have significant expertise in any one functional area: sales, product, marketing, customer success. In each discipline, we have experienced executives who have been there, done that several times over.

I constantly rely on my sphere to gain insight and advice from other experts to help guide my thinking, both inside and outside the company. Like the talented founders I respect, I try to surround myself with people who are smarter and more experienced than I am. And naturally, I put them in my Contactually buckets. Contactually the product has helped provide structure to something I was doing informally (and not that well) before.

I can honestly say nearly all of my personal growth—and much of our success as a business—has been a direct result of these relationships.

Social Capital

In Chapter 1, we discussed that *Homo sapiens* are naturally predisposed to seek social inclusion. We seek a sense of belonging. Value is also transferred through having social capital. You have likely witnessed, firsthand or through others, how having a certain social ranking can unlock value. The social standing may in and of itself be valuable. While I've typically shunned any environ that bears the moniker "VIP" or "see and be seen," one can't help but desire the *eligibility*.

Having people think highly of you matters. Your social capital is, essentially, your reputation. While this is not as quantitative as money or business growth, it often leads to both.

Feeling Good

Sometimes it just feels good. Having friends feels good. Doing something nice feels good. The moment you send that "Congratulations!" or "Thank you!" e-mail, you get this rush of pure joy, right? Dopamine, friends.

Many of you are reading this book to determine how to grow your business, advance your career, and increase your bank balance, clear indicators of "success" in our society. However, it's worth running our head through the mental gymnastics to determine whether we should root ourselves in that reality, or whether we truly possess a different definition of success.

CALCULATE YOUR ROI

You may be wondering, if I were to spend my time on relationship marketing, can I calculate the results I could achieve?

To do that, you can examine your current business and then calculate the potential lift of better leveraging your relationships. Alternatively, you can identify what your goal is, and then calculate what you would need from your relationships in order to achieve that. We're going to go with the former, as that is more straightforward.

1. Start with What You Have

Let's start by examining your current situation. You're not start-ing from zero, most likely. Based on the goals you want to achieve (usually split among closing new business, getting referrals, and working with existing customers), you already have some traction. So ask yourself the following questions:

- How many referrals do I get in a year?

- How many customers do I have? How many of them will work with me the following year?

- How many people are sending me referrals?

- How many people do I have in my network who are impor-tant to me?

2. Identify the Value of a Relationship

Eek, the value of a person? Reread the section in this chapter that addresses the "icky" factor. Remember, we are building a business, and the people associated with our business will help grow it.

- How much is a customer worth to me?

- How likely is a referral going to turn into a customer? (This is commonly referred to as your *conversion rate*.)

- How likely is a lead going to turn into a customer?

- What is the value of an individual contact in my network? (This is the fuzziest, but ask yourself how much you'd pay to be connected to that person.)

3. Calculate Lift, and Determine the Difference

This is where you identify what spending more time on your relationships will net you. Come up with an idea of the actual improvement from your actions. You can either produce estima-tions based on your activity (I will engage with 10 people a day that I would not otherwise) or market data. For example, we have seen from our users that effectively leveraging your relationships through software yields a 40 percent increase in referrals.

So your ROI would be:

(Value of a Referral) × (1 + .40) = _____

Looking at our user data, people see a 97 percent increase in the size of their active network.

So your ROI would be:

(Value of a Relationship) × (1 + 0.97) = _____

KEY TAKEAWAYS

- To develop a strategy to nurture your sphere of influence, you first have to determine what success would look like. What will you receive for your investment of time, money, and resources?

- You should not feel uncomfortable seeking personal and professional growth from the people you want to be close with professionally. It's a two-way street.

- To determine what success is, think about the different purposes of relationship marketing and what is more important to you.

- Be clear about what the potential outputs are. Money may initially come to mind as the primary objective. However, success isn't always measured in dollar signs.

CHAPTER 4

THE CAPITAL STRATEGY FOR MANAGING YOUR RELATIONSHIPS

You're uncorking yet another bottle of champagne (or cava, because I'm cheap and don't really care about the country of origin) at 11:30 p.m. on December 31. Partially aided by the combination of alcohol and sugar in the bubbles, you can't help but be excited by the new year. It's an opportunity to turn over a new leaf, you think. To achieve all the things you didn't get to in the waning year. To be a better version of yourself. Then again, maybe it's also the liquid confidence you're imbibing. As you count down the minutes, you set some fresh intentions for how you want to act over the course of the year.

We've seen this movie before. While December 31 may be a time of jubilation, January 1 comes around . . . and we'll get to it tomorrow. Then next week. Then next month. Our gym membership card hangs off our keychain, unused.

Resolutions are meaningless. Strategic plans win.

I cannot emphasize enough how important it is to have a strategic approach with your sphere of influence. But what does a strategy consist of? Relationship marketing, like most business activities, requires three key components: people, processes, and systems.

PEOPLE

Relationship marketing is the act of building and maintaining one-on-one relationships. You want people to know *you*, not necessarily the corporate entity you're representing. Keep in mind that our intent throughout is to build *personal, authentic relationships*. Technology can empower you, but it cannot replace you. The skills and activities will be laid out for you, but it requires *you* to turn the crank—that means sending a message, prioritizing your sphere of influence, and investing in the right people.

PROCESSES

Imagine if, every time you got into the car, you had to figure out how to turn the car on and drive.

Processes are the recipes that you develop to allow consistent and effective execution of relationship marketing tasks. Just like driving becomes a string of subconscious actions put together to get you to your desired destination, these relationship marketing processes are specific micro-tactics you use.

Hopefully, these become well-worn neural pathways, to the point where you can almost subconsciously execute when triggered. You know what notes you want to record during a meeting. You know how to do the research. You know how to write a good follow-up.

SYSTEMS

If we have the people and the knowledge of what steps we are going to take (processes), then systems are the tools that can enable and even supercharge your activities.

As we see across every aspect of our lives, technology is infiltrating the human experience. In many cases, it serves as a disruptor, slowly removing error-prone people from the equation. It changes who and how we interact with the world around us and each other. But more often than not, it helps us be better versions of ourselves. In the context of relationship marketing, we must eliminate the notion that technology *removes* us from interacting with our sphere of influence. Rather, technology can aid us in our activities. Let's think of it as the badass exoskeleton that Sigourney Weaver wears in *Aliens*.[1] With it, you can crush your tasks.

PAYTON STIEWE, REALTOR

Payton Stiewe started his career in sales and business development in the early Internet boom of the 1990s, before switching to real estate and becoming one of the top-producing agents in the San Francisco Bay Area.

While at Pacific Union, one of the largest brokerages in the region, I used Contactually to reach out to a client that I wouldn't have contacted otherwise, as the client wasn't in my region. Because I did, they got a $2.5 million listing. I look like a superhero.

Systems are not limited purely to technology. Systems are tools that help us, the *people*, better execute the *processes* in our strategy.

People, processes, and systems come together to form a perfect union, allowing you to execute consistently, effectively, and easily.

When we say people, that's you, my friend! You are the one leading the charge with these relationships. And I want to focus on the most important aspect—actually doing the work.

INTRODUCING:
THE CAPITAL STRATEGY

It's about time that we pull back the literary curtain and introduce you to the core strategy of the book. This has come through understanding the best (and worst) practices of thousands of professionals. Drawing on that, we've built and delivered software that aids professionals in their relationship marketing activities. That begat training and best practices, which begat this book, which begat Jacob and Esau. Whoops, wrong book.

I'm going to break down relationship marketing into seven key components and give a quick summary of each.

If you want to actively engage with specific sets of people to yield specific outcomes, you need *strategy*. All of these steps link together to help you nurture your sphere.

I'm not going to give you a specific recipe where any deviation means failure. I'm going to lay out the general recipe, the areas where you can deviate, and expected outcomes. From there, it's up to you to figure out what works for *you*. Here's a simple acrostic:

- **C**onsistent execution

- **A**ggregate

- **P**rioritize

- **I**nvestigate

- **T**imely engagement

- **A**dd value

- **L**everage

(Yes, this is a mnemonic. What kind of business book would this be without at least one mnemonic?) What you're trying to do is build up that all-important relationship capital, and the CAPITAL system of relationship marketing is your strategy to achieve it.

The subsequent chapters will explore each component in detail, but here's a brief description.

Consistent execution. Executing consistently is *the* most important thing to do to achieve the long-term objective. Your ability to break out of the urgent-response world and dedicate time to eventual outcomes will benefit you. We'll talk about how to engineer this habit.

Aggregate. Building and maintaining a strong database gives you a baseline from which to work. Leveraging today's technology, you can create a digital representation of everyone you know—and knew.

Prioritize. Not everyone will help you with your goals. Who will, and how important are they? We're not going to organize the chaos of your professional sphere; we're going to prioritize who is likely to help you move forward.

Investigate. People do business with people they know, so getting better at extracting and storing information on your prioritized relationships will give you working materials for the future.

Timely engagement. If mindshare decays, the simple solution is to have a periodic fallback pattern in case you don't connect for a specific reason. You'll build systems and practices for maintaining cadence, never letting prioritized relationships fade.

Add value. It's not just about following up. To make sure you're unforgettable, you want to deliver value. Guess what? Sending clients a fruitcake won't cut it.

Leverage. A critical way to ensure consistent behavior is to make it easier to execute the tasks themselves. That's where we seek to gain leverage.

Pop Quiz! CAPITAL. Can you remember what each letter stands for? Good.

I've laid out a relatively straightforward recipe that, in all likelihood, you can reflect on and easily understand. Each ingredient builds on those that come before it. To prioritize and collect intelligence, you need to have a method and practice for gathering all these relationships into a central place—aggregation. To deliver value, you need to have prioritized whom to focus on and determined the right time window for maximum impact. And *none* of this will matter at all if you spend all of your time responding to e-mail and putting out fires, or if you only act on this sporadically, say every six months. Consistent execution is the magic pill.

As we dive into each of these concepts, little should be particularly groundbreaking. Yet the simplest ideas typically have the greatest impact when executed well and consistently. Professionals have been practicing relationship marketing for decades or much longer. However, these practices aren't necessarily taught; they're passed down individually or learned over years of experience. It's frustrating to know that while relationship building is such an asset, it's rare to find a university, business school, or law school that teaches these tactics. We're trying to change that, to capture these ideas and best practices for your benefit.

We're going to jump into the first point now: Consistent execution. While the steps aren't incredibly complex, I want to warn you that consistent execution is challenging. As you lay out your strategy, you must keep this in mind. It's easy to accept the idea that "delivering value to your relationships will benefit you." It's a much harder challenge to figure out what to say to the right person at the right time and to execute on that knowledge.

KEY TAKEAWAYS

- Having a strategic focus is the solution to the scattered and faulty approach we naturally take to stay in touch.

- People, processes, and systems have to work in concert to aid you.

- Use the CAPITAL (Consistent execution, Aggregate, Prioritize, Investigate, Timely engagement, Add value, and Leverage) strategy for relationship marketing.

CHAPTER 5

CONSISTENT EXECUTION: SETTING UP THE RIGHT HABITS SO YOU CAN PLAY THE LONG GAME

> *We are what we repeatedly do. Excellence,*
> *then, is not an act, but a habit.*
> **—WILL DURANT**

If you were to take only one part of the CAPITAL strategy to heart and read only one chapter, it would be this one. Proper implementation and resilience around this one topic can be *the* key to untold success with your relationships.

While this is a seemingly simple theory in concept, the *actual execution is incredibly challenging.* As we discussed, one of the barriers to maintaining relationships is that your mind usually puts the long-term benefits of any task on the back shelf, so anything that doesn't help you right now is less likely to get done, especially if it has to be done repetitively. Modern technology will also more likely interrupt us than help us with that goal. Thus, being intentional is all the more important.

I'm pleading with you to take this to heart and end this chapter having implemented at least one of these tactics.

So, back to the CAPITAL strategy.

CAPITAL

The C stands for Cookie, and that's good enough for me. Wait, that's *Sesame Street*. C is for Consistent execution.

The CAPITAL strategy requires people, process, and systems. Of the three, which is the most likely to fail? I'll give you a hint: 80 percent of commercial airline accidents are due to pilot error, not bad planes or system failure.

You are the weakest link. *Your* weakness at doing the same repetitive task continuously over months and years, with no clear outcome, is the problem.

You need to ensure that your approach to relationship marketing is executed *consistently* over years. *You* need to build a habit.

THE VALUE OF HABIT

Good relationships develop over months and years, not days and weeks. So if you're serious about building a strong network or sphere, this is not something you can just do once and be done with. Nor is this a skill that you can just build up to in 10,000 hours and "have."

In Chapter 1, we discussed that strong relationships are extremely helpful for business generation and retention. Knowing the right people can lead to increased referrals, repeat business, and new opportunities. There are two challenges to that. First, there is a high level of unpredictability as to *when* a new opportunity might be generated from a certain relationship, if at all. Because there is usually no immediate reward from relationship-building activities, you have to focus on the long-term benefits. As we discussed in Chapter 2, that's a pretty big hill to climb.

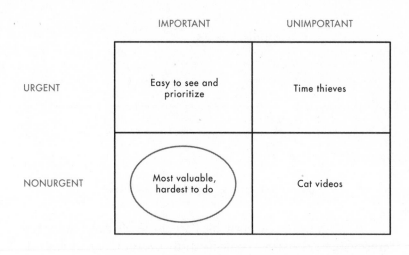

It is hard to focus on the long-term benefits.

The further out the reward, the less inclined we are to do the actions that generate it.

Houston, we have a problem. We are then, by nature, unlikely to invest our time continuously in relationship-building activities. But we know:

- That deal you just closed: there's a high likelihood that client will be in the market again in 5 years and unquestionably so in the next 10 years.

- That prospect you just met with: she's not ready to move forward yet, but could be in 2, 3, or 12 months.

- That person who came in for an interview: while he may not be a fit right now, he could be a strong candidate with two more years of experience and maturity.

- That introduction you just received: she didn't respond to the first e-mail but might after the second or third.

There is gold at the end of the rainbow, so how do we enable ourselves to get there?

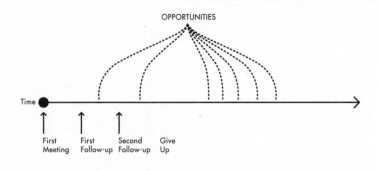

Opportunities come as a relationship progresses.

That's why we talk about habit. If we can implement the behavioral change necessary to execute with *any* regularity, we will set ourselves up for that longer-term benefit.

Let's relate this to other habitual activities society (and science) prescribes for us.

- Eating healthful foods

- Exercising regularly

- Reading

- Brushing and flossing

Don't get me wrong. All of these aforementioned activities have *some* short-term benefit. If you don't believe me, try having a light salad for lunch one day, and a burger and fries the next day. How do you feel in the early afternoon? Point made.

Even relationship building has some short-term benefit. Given our social predisposition, the act of interpersonal connection does check a psychological box for us. We usually feel good after talking to someone, more so if we are engaging with a past relationship. If nothing else, we checked something off our list, and at least tried.

However, the *larger balance* of value reciprocated from these best practices happens over the long term. Compare the guy who's eaten fast food his entire life with the woman who watches her diet and intake. You can safely assume that there is a canyon-sized gap in health and quality of life.

To implement that behavioral change so we can regularly invest time in our relationships with the end zone in mind, we need to build that *habit*.

What Habits Do You Have?

You have many habits that you may not even notice, as you're primarily operating subconsciously. You've repeated those actions so often that you're set in your ways. Rarely have I left the house without my wallet, smartphone, and keys. The neural pathways are so well worn that it takes little to no effort.

When it comes to *conscious, intentional* habits, I would venture to guess you don't have as many as you would like.

Brushing your teeth is the first one that comes to mind. There are bigger habits, like getting dressed, eating, going to work, but it's hard to call those habits as much as basic survival tactics in a modern society. I'm sure you've tried to establish other habits—waking up early to meditate, going to the gym, flossing . . . Why is it so hard?

The type of habits we're focusing on are ones in which the outcome or desire is detached from daily action. How many times have you fallen asleep trying to meditate? Flossing doesn't seem to provide real benefit to us immediately (unless you're a model). The friction of going to the gym, working out, and smelling like a wet sock doesn't seem to make it worthwhile to us until six months later when we've got that beach bod.

Professional relationships are the same in that regard. We have to realize that sending that one e-mail, connecting with that one person, or doing our research won't provide any immediate yield. When a multitude of those discrete actions are summed over long time periods, that's where we see definite benefits.

CUE, ROUTINE, REWARD

Nir Eyal, author of *Hooked*, defines a habit simply as a behavior performed with little to no conscious thought. Charles Duhigg, author of *The Power of Habit* breaks down habits into three major steps: cue, routine, and reward. The cue is what triggers the behavior and could be anything from a visual element to the company of a certain person. The routine is the habit itself, the behavior that you've learned to perform unconsciously. The reward is the feeling you get after performing the routine, often a positive emotional response, which strengthens the habit.

The reason it can be so hard to kick a bad habit is because of this reward. Take smokers, who are rewarded with a nicotine rush as they take that first drag. If they try to break this habit, they'll be denied the reward that comes with it, which often elicits a negative emotional response, varying in intensity depending on how strong the habit is. That's why it's so hard to quit smoking.

But how does a habit form in the first place? According to Duhigg, the root is found in chunking, "in which the brain converts a sequence of actions into an automatic routine." This only occurs after the behavior has been repeated a number of times.

Once a habit is established, it's stored within the basal ganglion, a small but vital portion of your brain. Our brain is capable of storing automatic routines—if only we are able to program it.

So the cycle we want to get into consistently is:

- Get triggered to do the relationship-building activity.
- Do the relationship marketing work.
- Feel rewarded.

GETTING OFF THE COUCH AND DOING THE THING

I work out at 5 a.m. every day. The intensity of my morning workout may vary. It could be as light as yoga or stretching, a grueling session on the spin bike, or weightlifting. The actual gym activity is not the hardest part of my mornings. As you can likely relate to, the hardest part is the mental decision I have to make at 5 a.m. to leave the comfort of being horizontal, knowing that the alternative to my bed is physical torture. Acting on that trigger to get myself moving is a challenge.

No routine, no software, no immediate or future reward will matter if you don't take that first step—again and again. Treat relationship marketing as a habit that you must build.

Here are two hacks that will help you.

Hack #1: The Recurring Calendar Appointment

The likelihood that you, aspiring business professional, use a calendar to drive your work day is pretty high. You've already built the habit of looking at your calendar every morning and after every appointment to determine what you have to do next. So if there is something that you want to do every day, it might make sense for you to have it on that calendar. *If it's not scheduled, it's not getting done.*

It's not my place to dictate to you exactly when to do it, nor for how long. There is enough variance in the structure of our day, when we're at our highest and lowest energy levels,[1] and when we are more or less likely to get interrupted with something valid enough to switch tasks. To determine the best time of day or week, consider:

- Do you find yourself freshest and at peak energy and focus in the morning? Or are you more dialed in during late afternoons or evenings, once you've conquered the day?

- Flip back through your calendar the previous few weeks. Were there any consistent gaps in your schedule? For me, Friday mornings are always the quietest, so I use the time for my own relationship marketing.

- The frequency is up to you, as long as it is regular and consistent. If you are able to build a daily habit, go for it. Dialing it back to short blocks three times a week could work just as well. You also might be wired for batching, blocking off a longer period of time once a week. When you're trying to maintain a relationship over a long time

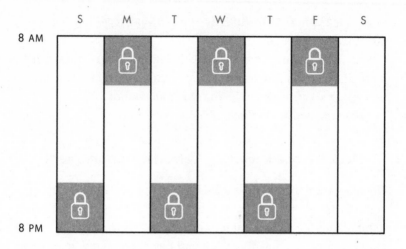

Schedule relationship-building activities in your calendar.
Lock in those times, free from other distractions.

horizon and trying to catch up once a quarter, whether you choose to engage them on a Wednesday morning or a Friday afternoon will not be of any noticeable difference to them, especially when compared to not doing it at all.

- As a starting point, put in a recurring (repeating) calendar event, usually in the morning. Avoid scheduling it so early that you won't actually do it, or so late in the morning that you're already swept up in the day. You may also schedule it for the end of the day, before you go home.

Commit to this being your time. Don't sacrifice it to other meetings. Defend it with your life!

How Much Time Do You Need?

How much time should you set aside? I've seen many successful professionals who have wildly different approaches; especially when it comes to the pure *amount* of time they are investing into their sphere. How many people are you trying to engage with? How deeply do you invest in these relationships? These are topics we'll cover in much more depth in the coming chapters.

- It takes 20 minutes to find and buy a gift.

- Ten minutes to handwrite and mail a card.

- Five minutes to write an e-mail.

- One minute to send a text message.

- One minute to find and comment on an online post.

How many of these actions are you going to be doing within a week?

I recommend *one hour* a day. Within this hour, one has the ability to accomplish a mix of the aforementioned actions. *How* you fill the time and with *whom* will be discussed in later chapters.

PATRICK EWERS, EXECUTIVE AND RELATIONSHIP MARKETING COACH

Ever feel like there just isn't enough time in the day? Like after you finish responding to e-mails, replying to Slack messages, and sitting in meetings, there's no time left for your network?

You aren't alone.

Time management is one of the most universal challenges faced by people across the world, especially entrepreneurs. And it isn't helped by the fact that our lives are becoming increasingly reaction-driven.

- New e-mail? Gotta respond immediately.
- Slack message? Better get on that right away.
- Meeting request? Can't turn that down.

It's easy to spend a whole day on supposedly urgent, reactive tasks only to get to the end and realize you didn't actually *accomplish* anything. Sure, you responded to 62 e-mails. But was that really the *best* use of your time? The most *productive*? Probably not.

The truth is, you're never going to *"find time"* to invest in your relationships. You have to *make it.* And while there are countless great time management strategies out there, the best I've found is Whitespace Time.

At its core, Whitespace Time is simply calendar blocking. It means blocking off a two- to four-hour chunk of time *each week* solely dedicated to those high-level tasks that often get put off but end up making the biggest impact, such as proactively managing your relationships.

Once scheduled—*go ahead and do it now, I'll wait*—the key is treating Whitespace sessions with absolute priority: short of an emergency, *nothing* gets scheduled over them—after all, it's one of the most important parts of your week. Act accordingly.

Try This: Yes, the Hour of Power

At whatever cadence you feel comfortable—daily, three times a week, weekly—block off an hour in your calendar and label it in all caps, HOUR OF POWER. This is, to invoke the standard cliché, your time to work *on* your business, not *in* your business. Ignore e-mails that come in, phone calls (unless it's a return call), or any other task. You're in proactive mode, not reactive mode. I'm not kidding around when I tell you that, more than any other tactic or strategy this book contains, the successful implementation and adherence to a regular Hour of Power will unlock long-term opportunity building that can level up your business.

Hack #2: Association

When I leave the house in the morning, it's rare that I walk out with empty pockets. That's because I've built the habit of grabbing my phone, wallet, and keys. I've *associated* filling my pockets as something I have to do every time I *leave the house.*

B. J. Fogg is a behavioral psychologist, author, and founder of Stanford Behavior Design Lab. In his excellent Tiny Habits course,[2] he teaches you to think of a trigger you have that you're already regularly doing in your day, and associating a new habit with that, either immediately before or immediately after.

Study the specifics of your daily routine, and where you could potentially insert something new:

- Waking up

- Feeding your pet

- Turning on your phone

- Walking into the office

- Logging on to your computer

- Getting that first cup of coffee

- Eating lunch

- Packing up for the day

- Walking into the house

Building a new habit could be as easy as memorizing:

After I _____, I'll spend five minutes working on my network.

Note that, as opposed to the hour block of time, I've winnowed it down to just five minutes. Part of the success of B.J.'s formula centers on making the initial task as easy and simple as possible, so just getting started will pull you into the full task (learn more about the Zeigarnik effect[3]).

We've observed the following to be successful paths:

- Once you get to the office, after you've checked e-mail for the first time

- Before your first cup of coffee (coffee becomes a reward!)

- Before you leave for the day

Try it!

We Should Probably Talk About Working with an Assistant

We're going to talk more about leveraging assistants and virtual assistants in a later chapter. However, I do want to plant the idea in your head now that one way of implementing habit is by relying on a human/cyborg third party, in the form of an in-office or virtual assistant to aid in repeated tasks.

FALLING OFF THE WAGON

Let's be honest. Whatever good habits you have—or are trying to build—you will miss a day. And that day can become two days, and then three days. Then three weeks. Then two months. Then . . . will you ever get back to it?

You've undoubtedly been through this cycle many times, as have I. You know that breaking a streak of good work starts off as an honest mistake, or you simply just didn't have the energy for it. Reasonable situations. Going back to the gym analogy, you may have hurt a muscle, gotten a cold, or been traveling. That breaks your otherwise groundbreaking three-day streak of working out every day, and you swear you'll pick it back up tomorrow. But as time goes on, that quickly turns to guilt. Just like the mess you have in your garage, it feels better to ignore it than to address it.

This is something we see *constantly*. While it doesn't really matter whether you follow up with someone today or tomorrow or next week, the fact that you know there's an ever-increasing pile of people you should be engaging with or tasks to complete makes it even harder to pick back up.

It's safe to say in this day and age that quitting smoking has a dramatically positive impact on the life of the smoker. Research has shown that it can take up to *30* attempts before a smoker successfully quits for one year or longer.[4] It's in the smoker's best interest to keep trying until he or she has finally kicked the addiction. If establishing a good habit like relationship marketing is anything like quitting smoking, it may take you as many attempts. What matters more than failure is the ability to pick back up.

So What Do You Do If You Break Your Habit?

- Realize that "falling off the wagon" is completely OK.

- While most people may use that as an excuse to lose the habit—and forgo any benefits that come from it forever—you have the opportunity to be the person who does pick it back up.

- Right when you're thinking of it—and don't delay any further—do one small tiny action that helps you get back on track—something that you can do in a few seconds or minutes. This can be as simple as sending one e-mail to someone you haven't spoken to in a while.

This can help you pierce the guilt barrier and get you back into the flow.

Contactually nearly failed to launch because of this very issue. When it started out as a side project, we were always struggling to get back to working on it, as we were focused on our day jobs. So occasionally, a week or two would go by with nothing happening. But instead of it just lying fallow forever, we would pick it back up—even for just a few minutes a day—which got us back into the swing of things.

DOING THE WORK

Consistent and regular triggers are the lifeblood of developing consistency when building relationships. Heeding the right triggers is not the entire aspect of relationship building. There is *doing the work* and the *reward*.

The habit gurus Nir Eyal, B. J. Fogg, and Charles Duhigg would all agree on one key point: *The harder the work is, the less likely you are to repeatedly execute.*

Going back to my gym example: If I felt the same walking out of the gym regardless of how much work I do, I'm much less likely to get out of bed if I'm expecting 90 minutes of "hell" versus 20 minutes of easy cardio. Not a perfect analogy as I know that some of you masochists love a "challenge" or know there's no way you can walk out of 90-minute gym session without an endorphin high, but for the rest of us mere mortals, the harder the gym routine is, the less inclined we will be to do this consistently.

This translates well into our relationship marketing activities. The easier we make it to practice our relationship marketing tactics, the greater the chance we have of executing consistently.

What does *easier* mean?

It can't take a lot of time. Time is our scarcest resource, and it feels like we have less and less of it. The bigger the hole in our calendar, the more we may sacrifice it to more time-sensitive concerns.

It should not be mentally challenging. Your cognitive attention is also limited. We want to make it as easy as possible to do, like microwaving a frozen pizza instead of making a *haute cuisine* quiche from scratch.

Repetition should be minimal. You'll want to spend your time doing what you do best; original thought and action, so if it can be automated or templated, it should be.

It has to be the right amount of work for you, at the right time. The relationship marketing practices of a recent college grad and a 55-year-old rainmaker will be similar in theory, but *very* different in practice. Do not be afraid to mentally shelve many of the more advanced tactics for now; they'll be there for you when you're ready. Start simple. For some, that might be as basic as pulling a random contact out of your phone or LinkedIn profile and sending a three-line "how's-yer-ma" message. *We're cheering you for doing that!*

Tune your efforts over time. Start small and build from there.

REWARDING YOURSELF

I have placed almost *too* much emphasis on the reward being in the long-term value of a healthy relationship with a key business

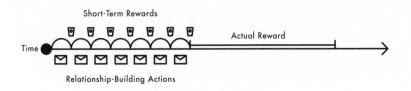

Use short-term rewards for motivation.

professional. I'll still defend that, but I'm also totally aware that there are plenty of short-term benefits that could arise. Maybe there is an instantaneous response to a message with a business opportunity. Sometimes the response itself, "Good to hear from you!" can evoke a positive feeling. Let's internalize that the act of relationship building and knowing that we are being social and connecting with others is a reward in itself.

I want to overcompensate for the level of our efforts here and operate under the assumption that we won't gain *any* benefit in the short term from the work we do.

For that reason, I completely support developing artificial rewards for our short-term efforts, knowing that the long-term value will more than compensate for their cost. Yes, I'm saying that buying yourself that really expensive frozen mochaccino, taking yourself out to lunch, or eating some chocolate is OK. Give yourself a reward after, say, sending 10 messages to people you know. The reward is the last step of the trigger-routine-reward cycle. The more you feel rewarded, the more likely the demons of laziness resting in your subconscious will be kept at bay the next time that trigger is fired. They know that something fun is coming.

Ideas?

- Small food or drink reward.

- Short break: you've earned those cat videos!

- Place a few dollars aside for a vacation—in a prominent and visible (yet safe) place.

Ensuring that you feel rewarded for doing the right thing in the short term will help enable your efforts in the long term.

GETTING TACTICAL

- Determine the time of day, days of the week, and amount of time per session you're able to dedicate to proactively engaging and adding value to your sphere of influence.

- Set a recurring calendar appointment as appropriate in whatever calendar tool you use. If nothing else, set alarms on your phone triggering you to take action.

- Alternatively, if you want to break it up into much smaller tasks, associate it with something you already do, such as after you check your e-mail in the morning or right before you shut down your computer for the day.

- Determine a consistent, immediate-gratification reward for whenever you accomplish the task, something as small as watching funny cat videos.

QUICK WIN

Block off a recurring one-hour block every Monday, Wednesday, and Friday, and call that your Hour of Power.

KEY TAKEAWAYS

- Humans are wired to think in the short term, so we have to be intentional in changing our behaviors to repeatedly exert effort in building our relationships.

- Having the right trigger to get us started can help, a recurring calendar appointment or associating it with something we already do regularly.

- While we want to act consistently, the worst thing we can do is stumble and stop entirely. Build up your resilience, and don't feel bad if you drop the habit. Just start again!

- The easier your routines are, the more likely you are to repeat them.

- Intentionally reward yourself so you are more likely to repeat the actions in the future.

CHAPTER

6

AGGREGATE: BUILDING YOUR SPHERE

We've set our sights on the ultimate goals we seek to achieve. We've laid the foundation of your overall relationship marketing efforts: being consistent in your behavior over the long term. To prioritize your relationships, add value to them, and systematize your efforts to engage, we need to know who these people are—not just from a superficial name/contact perspective but on a deeper level. In this chapter, we're going to lay out tactics to get that broad and deep database in order.

If relationships are a core asset to your business, you should be treating your database the same way you do your bank account. Just like a bank account, the balance can rise and fall, which you directly control. But first, let's find out how much we have.

To start, we have to be clear what we're talking about when referring to "relationships" in our database.

WHAT'S A CONTACT?
WHAT'S A RELATIONSHIP?

In the realm of database building and intelligence, *relationships* are far more important than *contacts*.

A *contact* is simply the identifiers for a person. Name, phone number, e-mail address.

A relationship, though, is the real asset we're building. A *relationship* is your connection to the person. How you know people, why they're important, what your goal is with them, the history of your relationship, their favorite flavor of ice cream. A relationship is their connection back to you as well. If all they are to you is a contact—name, rank, serial number—that is meaningless. Contacts are worth nothing more than the paper stock the business card is printed on. Relationships, however, can be of infinite value.

When it comes to approaching our database, the base record may just be the contact: first name, last name, e-mail address, phone. Even getting *that* may be a challenge, but there's no real value in just that. It does serve, however, as the foundation for what you are looking to achieve. The base contact is mere data, and data is a commodity these days. Contact information and information surrounding that contact are bought and sold freely in software networks around the world. Doing a quick web search for yourself exposes some of that, but that's the tip of the iceberg. If average consumers fully understood how much information about them is stored by the likes of Experian, LiveRamp, or Oracle Marketing Cloud, they'd be throwing their ID and credit cards into the backyard grill and living the rest of their lives off the grid. You can find tons of services that will get you anyone's contact information. It's freely available in their e-mail signatures and on their business cards. Just collecting that, whether in a social network or an application you own, is like throwing *pennies in a jar*. The only real value you have so far is that the contact is there in the first place, giving you some hint that this person could have once been or could still be of some importance to you.

If your database becomes your source of information on the *relationships* you have with your contacts, however, then you have an invaluable asset.

That's why we should think about making it as easy as possible to capture the *contact*, so we can focus our time on tracking, building, and maintaining those *relationships*.

BUILDING YOUR DATABASE

If you're more than 50 years old, you remember your Rolodex being a key item on your desk at work and kitchen counter at home, always within arm's reach. If you're younger than 50, ask your parents or grandparents if they recall using one. I'm sure it's hidden somewhere. Regardless of shape or "technology" like dust shields, it still held the same information: who you know.

That was back when there were essentially two methods of contact: people's phone number and their postal address. You called them, wrote them a letter, or went to their house. Remember the fax machine? That was the latest technology at one point.

OK, enough strolling down memory lane to the good old days of corded telephones when you had as many relationships as you did paper index cards.

Today there is a proliferation of channels through which to engage people, methods of communication, and repositories where information about these relationships are stored. Your database must reflect how we can and must work today, not how we did things yesterday.

CHOOSING YOUR DATABASE

If you were to walk down any street in New York City and ask each bystander where the best slice of pizza in Manhattan is, you will get a wide variety of answers. And they are all right: it's the best slice of pizza *for them*. Everyone has their own tastes, background, experiences, desired sauce levels, etc.

There are many different tools you can leverage to assist you in aggregating your relationships. It could be as simple as a spreadsheet. You could use a full-blown automation platform. Customer relationship management (CRM) software is such an incredibly broad category.

It might even be a giant whiteboard or stacks of business cards. Don't laugh, I've seen those systems work for some people.

The purpose of a database is to have something that represents who you know and the relationships you have with them. That gives you a lot of leeway. This is also where you are looking to better map to the goals you are trying to achieve.

WHY I STARTED CONTACTUALLY

There are a number of big ideas behind Contactually, but the initial impetus came from me needing to aggregate my relationships— and the challenges I was facing in consistently doing so.

While I was a consultant, I gained a deep appreciation for how relationships and reputation drive a business forward. For years, my sources of business were my relationships and my reputation, allowing me to work on projects for industry leaders at the time, including Ford Motors, CBS Interactive, the New York Stock Exchange, and more. Keeping track of these relationships as their priority and urgency ebbed and flowed in importance turned out to be my biggest sales challenge. Knowing that I could definitely improve on this by systematizing it, I looked for software solutions to solve the problem.

As I tried various solutions, I found one common problem. It's a complaint I've heard echoed by many different types of professionals.

It's too much work.

That is true, to a point. It isn't that it's too much work per se; it's that it's too much work *relative to the value provided.* When all you get is an empty container, a blank database in which to put your information manually, the onus is entirely on you to fill it. And keep it updated. And keep it clean. And keep it updated. The moment you *stop* updating it, the moment it no longer reflects reality, it becomes completely useless.

The eureka moment was pretty simple: Most or all of the information (at least the baseline interaction information) was easily accessible. We communicate via e-mail, and most mail servers have standard application programming interfaces (API). An API is the route through which the developer of an application will define how information residing in that application can be extracted or changed. APIs are used by our calendars, many social networks, and even some phones. So if we *can* get all the information on who we're talking to, why don't our CRMs do that? What if there were a *proactive CRM* that searched and got all the needed information? It wouldn't necessarily be the same *garbage in, garbage out* issue that older databases suffer from because it would reflect reality closer than anything else, a reality that is as honest and messy as the real world.

Contactually was born.

WHAT SHOULD I THINK ABOUT IN CHOOSING WHAT TO USE?

The core question is: *Will I use it*? But it goes much deeper than that. In the previous chapter, we spoke about habit and consistency. When we broke it down, effective habit is a mix of trigger, ability, and reward. In order to effectively execute a task repeatedly, *ability* is about making sure it's as easy as possible to do relative to the trigger and reward. So, the question we need to have in our heads is: Will *I* use this? Not anyone else. Not your neighbor or colleague or friend. Not what someone mentioned in a Facebook thread. The best solution for you is the one that *you* will gain the most value from for the effort you are willing to put into it.

Ask yourself:

- Will this work with my contact sources?

- Does this work with all my other tools?

- Do I understand how to use it?

- Is this as rigid or flexible as I want it to be?

Two professionals may come up with very different answers to these questions, and therefore different solutions.

I am completely in support of whatever you are using successfully, and likewise strongly urge you to drop whatever you're not using successfully like that cup of extra-hot coffee you forgot to put a cardboard sleeve around. In our contemporary, find-a-digital-solution-for-everything world, I applaud and respect professionals who have made analog systems work—quite literally, writing their contacts on a whiteboard, or keeping stacks of business cards on their desk.

YOUR RELATIONSHIPS VERSUS YOUR COMPANY'S

Thinking back to your goals, having a sphere of influence is an important asset to *you*—not just to the company you work for, even if you're the head of it. Your relationships run deeper and have a shelf life beyond your current employer, so we highly recommend that you have a database that *you own*. Instead of just following what your company prescribes as its CRM practice, prioritize your *own* use case first, then determine how it can connect to any existing tools at your disposal.

You may be working in an organization where the company provides and requires the use of its CRM. This is typically the case

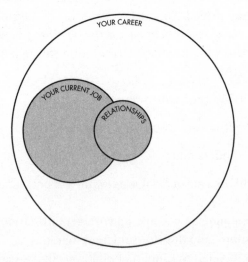

Your career and relationships extend beyond your current job.

in most sales organizations. The CRM can be the primary way of calculating how much you get paid, or if you have a job at all. Yikes! Keep in mind that not only does the company own the software, it also owns the information in it—even the information you entered yourself. You're best served by keeping your own database completely separate. Even if your company has some rules around your ability to later do business with people you've transacted with in your current role, they cannot *prevent you from knowing them*, which is why these people can and should be represented in your own database. This becomes all the more essential if, as an employee, you want to bring your old contacts with you to a new job.

YOU HAVE A DATABASE— WHAT NOW?

Aggregate. What an awful-sounding word. I am careful in the use of the term *aggregate*. Due to the nature of how we communicate—public networks, open standards, private protocols—our communications with people are everywhere. You have chat buddies, social network friends, e-mail recipients, phone contacts, and so many more. They will always be separate. So instead of trying to centralize those relationships, your focus should be on the *continual aggregation* into a central location. You will never have one "authoritative resource"; Social Network A will never listen to Messenger System C, which will never run off your smartphone provider contacts. So having one database—that you have full ownership and control over—where all of that information can flow into and reside, is important. I used the word *continual* on purpose above, not just because "who we know," "what can be known about them," and "what we're doing with them" are everchanging. We're also adding and removing people from these sources. The context around them may change, such as someone updating his or her title on LinkedIn or moving cities. If you were to do a one-time export of your e-mail contacts and drop them into a system, the moment one of them changes his or e-mail address,

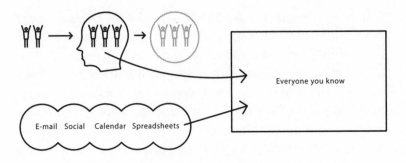

A database never forgets.

your database no longer reflects reality. We want our database to, with or without our help, be as current as possible as much of the time as possible.

Relationship marketing is a mix of people, process, and technology. The foundation of effective implementation of the strategy is maintaining Consistency, which we talked about in the previous chapter. Repetitive execution over a long time is the foundation on which we can build our strategy of specific tactics, then our database is the foundation of our technology approach. Our process and tactics will be run on top of our central database. For example, in order to prioritize relationships, you need to know which relationships you want to prioritize.

Should I Include My Personal Relationships?

Yes.

Ugh, but That Is a Lot of People— and a Lot of Irrelevant Contacts

Yes, your past clients will be mixed in with your plumber, and your top prospects with vendors. That's OK. Better to capture *too much* information than too little. *Your database should be a digital representation of reality.*

You want to include *everyone* you know, and everything you know about them.

A pristine database of only "relevant" people is a false idol. Someone who is relevant today may not be relevant tomorrow. So include everyone. The next step is to prioritize.

A Big Database Doesn't Necessarily Have to Mean a Messy One

For one of my birthdays as a teenager, I received four copies of Green Day's magnum opus, *Dookie*. Just because I loved the album, though, didn't mean I needed to keep every copy.

You may get a lot of copies of the same contact coming into your database, especially from automated systems. It's pretty easy for you (or whatever application you're using) to identify obvious duplicates based on a unique identifier (an e-mail address is best these days) and to reconcile conflicting data. We want our database to reflect reality, so if you know John Smith, then john.h.smith@skynet.gov and johnsmith@gmail.com should not be two separate contacts. This is where having a good application that handles the mess of de-duplication and merging will make us wonder how on earth people dealt with this before.

Your Database Should Have as Much Information as Possible

The cost of digital storage has gone down so dramatically over the past 20 years that we've all turned into digital packrats. The cost of retaining something we *might* need at some point decades from now is nothing compared to the relative opportunity cost of deleting it (as I write this, the industry average cost per gigabyte of data is around two cents), so that should put us at ease about having every contact and getting as much information as possible in our database.

What we do need to control, however, is the resource cost (your time and money) of proactively finding, understanding, and collecting insights on those relationships. We'll talk about that in a later chapter.

Through whatever sources you're retrieving your contacts from, you can pull in additional information beyond just first name, last name, and e-mail address. For example:

- Your database connecting to your mail server will show all the incoming and outgoing interactions you have with your contacts.

- Pulling in your calendar will show you where and when you've met them.

- LinkedIn may also provide their job title and company.

- FullContact or other data sources can do a quick scan of your database and find the social network profiles of your contacts.

Automate as Much as Possible; Schedule the Rest

This is where your selection of a database matters; simplifying the level of effort this task takes increases the likelihood that you actually achieve it. I'm going to keep bringing this up until you set this book or e-reader on fire, or, better yet, *buy it for all of your friends and colleagues.* Ensuring that your database represents the current reality of your sphere of influence with as little effort as possible will strengthen your ability to *use* the database.

Luckily, most of it can be automated. When I founded Contactually, a good chunk of my justification for pursuing it was that the information *could* be easily retrieved. The "Web 2.0" frenzy kicked off circa 2006[1] and resulted in the popularity of APIs allowing different software platforms to "talk" to each other and exchange information. For the purposes of this book, we don't need to go any further than saying that *our database can automatically update with information stored in other places.*

Here's what can, in most instances, be retrieved automatically.

- **E-mail conversations.** Almost every mail system has a public API through which information can be easily retrieved, unless you work in a high-security environment (or your risk-averse corporate IT feels like one). Almost every Gmail, Office365, or MS Exchange service supports that. If you're using something else, you can check with your provider to see if it supports IMAP or any other protocol. There is a high likelihood that, if you can use the native mail client on your smartphone, you can connect your e-mail account to your database.

- **Calendar events.** If you're using a web-hosted calendar (and not one that just resides in an application on your computer), you should be able to retrieve a *feed* of past and future events that your database, if supported, can pull in.

- **Phone contacts and more.** The address book in most smartphones can be read from, usually by installing an application from your database provider on that phone and granting permission to access it. In some cases (this is currently limited to phones running Android), those phone apps can also retrieve your incoming and outgoing phone calls and text messages.

- **Social networks.** While most don't, some social networks, such as Twitter, still believe in interoperability and will allow your database or other tools to access information on them.

Theoretically, then, our database can have an up-to-date record of every e-mail interaction, every meeting, and every call or text we engage in. That is incredible, right?

Other relevant information will require a little bit of manual effort to access.

- **Social networks.** LinkedIn, still the predominant network representing professional connections, unfortunately made the choice in 2014 to cut off third-party access to your information. However, you can export a spreadsheet, a table of text information stored as one or many lines, normally as a *comma-separated values* (*CSV*) file, which can then be imported into your database. Take note that some social networks, most notably Facebook, have made the unfortunate decision to block your ability to get *anything* out of their "walled garden," meaning that you will have to copy and paste every contact manually. WhatsApp? The same.

- **Other applications.** There are a limitless number of applications that may hold relevant information on your relationships. If your database says it supports them, you're golden and can follow its instructions. Otherwise, search to see if you're able to export your contacts in a format your database can read (most likely a CSV file). Your database may very well host an API, but that doesn't mean their developers have built an integration into it. It's always worth the ask.

For the ones from which you can manually export information, if you choose to, as part of your database cleanup ritual, *plan to export your contacts from those sources* into your database. The fact that most of those relationships are already in your database shouldn't matter; if you're using a modern database, it is likely smart enough to detect and gracefully handle duplicate data.

What Else Should We Be Putting in Our Database?

At zero or minimal cost to us, our database already has a pretty solid amount of information, which serves as context around the relationships.

But there is so much more information out there. And there is so much more that we can use to frame our relationships with our contacts, which can be used to deepen them.

- She's in our database, but what type of professional relationship do I have with her?

- He works at ACME. Is ACME a company I want to work with?

- We have her birthday, but do we know what her favorite kind of cake is?

- We know his current job title, but do we know if that's the job he wants?

- She lives in the New York City area, but does she have kids? And what are those kids into?

These are normal questions that elevate a contact from a phone number and e-mail address to an actual person you'd want to spend time and do business with. I don't want us to undervalue the information that the database has already aggregated, hopefully with little to no effort so far. But *for the people we really need to care about*, we'll be better served by rolling up our sleeves and seeking out those key insights.

We next need to take this hulking database, representing everyone we know, and add a narrowing filter to zero in on the relationships we believe will best deliver value that matches our goals.

GETTING TACTICAL

- Pick a database that works for you. It has to be something that you feel comfortable putting your personal relationships in, that works the way that you do, and that is easy enough that you can quickly understand how to use it.

- Get all of your contacts, conversations, and notes in there. Import your contacts from as many sources as possible: your e-mail accounts, phone, calendar, billing systems, other tools, and social media.

QUICK WIN

Connect your professional e-mail account to a web-based contact management system.

KEY TAKEAWAYS

- Your database is the technical foundation of your relationship marketing.

- Choose a database that reflects how *you* want to work.

- Your database should represent current reality as closely as possible.

- The more automated and easier it is to use, the better.

PRIORITIZE: HIGHLIGHTING THOSE IN YOUR NETWORK WHO CAN HELP

Over the course of our lives, we'll meet and interact with many people. Some may be fleeting encounters, the barista at the coffee shop, for example. Who should we retain? More important, who do we need to ensure *remembers us*?

We're going to spend this chapter exploring ways of thinking about the "who" part of your relationship management strategy and coming up with tactics for filtering through the noise.

WHO SHOULD I TALK TO TODAY?

It's easy to quickly assume one can easily identify which contacts are important; stick with me though. One of the biggest challenges we've seen our customers face is improper identification of which contacts are important and of what even constitutes important.

Your database is a digital store of everyone you've known. That means that it is *not* the definitive collection of everyone you *want* to know or everyone you want to know *you*. Those people, however, are almost certainly a subset of it. Nor is it the list of people

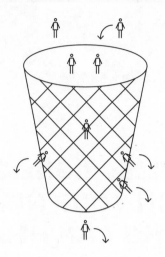

Who do we need to maintain a relationship with?

you should be keeping track of or talking to. Again, those people are a subset of your larger database. So if our database is the entire known universe of your sphere of influence, then you must add a filter to focus on which people *you choose* to engage with.

Prioritize Around Your Goals, Top to Bottom

Before we identify the buckets of people that we need to stay engaged with, we have to start with the why.

In an earlier chapter, we talked about setting your intention. Let's bring that back to the front of our mind. We're spending all of our time investing in our relationships for one (or multiple) of these reasons. This is by no means a definitive list, but this should cover 80 percent of professional uses of relationship management:

- Generating additional business opportunities
- Retaining existing business or generating repeat business
- Closing more business
- Networking
- Brand building

Great, so we have the why. Let's dig deeper.

What Types of People Are Going to Help Achieve These Goals?

It may take some time to think about it. I know we're tempted to say, "Gordon Gekko is someone who's going to help me close more business." But not only is he a fictional character, we haven't yet answered if he's the right type of person. So who are the types of people who could help us achieve these goals? These could be colleagues, vendors, past clients, college friends, or old girlfriends, but it's important to identify the types of people.

Now, who fits those types?

Great, now it's just a matter of filling the buckets. Who are my past clients? Who are my vendors?

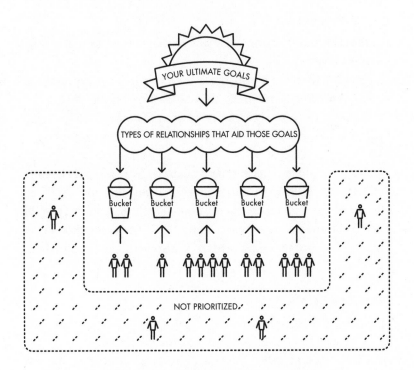

Which relationships can help you meet your goals?

Let's Walk Through Some Examples

To get the gears turning in your mind, let's bring up a few examples of how someone can start with a high-level goal, and end up with a clear idea of who they should be prioritizing.

I'm a Software Consultant Who Is Trying to Grow His Business

I care about closing more business. That's my high-level goal. (I have other goals in life, but let's keep it simple.)

If I want to close more business, then the types of people I need to stay in touch with are "Anyone I've met at coffee shops or events," "People I've sent proposals to," "Early stage start-ups," and "Designers."

OK, great. Now I just need to identify all the designers I know and put them in a bucket.

I'm an Accountant

I care about retaining my business year over year, as most of my business is seasonal.

If I want to retain my business, then I should capture all of the clients I've worked with in the last year as "Current clients."

Some of these are more important than others—the growing businesses, family accounts—so I want to have "High value clients" as well.

I also would like to get repeat business from people I haven't worked with recently, so "Past clients" is a good one, too.

I can export all recent clients from my billing system. I should also be able to retrieve my past clients. I can either filter though my current clients to pick out the high-value ones or go through them one by one.

I'm a Real Estate Agent

I want to get more referrals.

Who are the types of people who send me referrals?

Well, "Past clients," "Mortgage brokers," and "Out of town agents."

Looking for more? We have a whole set of potential buckets for you to think about in Appendix B.

PRIORITIZE, DON'T ORGANIZE

I love to cook. For 9 or 10 hours a day, I'm in the world of big-picture decisions, negotiations, research, putting out fires, and maintaining the facade of confidence and positivity a CEO needs to be wearing at all times. There is nothing better than coming home, putting all that aside, and just *creating*—which is what I do when I'm cooking. And because I cook all sorts of different cuisines, I've amassed a pretty overwhelming arsenal of spices on my counter. The people who think they can do everything with just salt, pepper, and maybe a bit of fresh garlic, I salute you.

Naturally, there are some spices I use a lot more than others: garlic powder, chili powder, salt, paprika. Those are right at the front of the shelf so I can grab them as needed. Some I use less regularly—chipotle, cumin, cinnamon—so they are usually just behind. Then the dozens of others I rarely use—coriander, saffron, ras el hanout (whatever that is)—are in the back. I'm prioritizing the items I constantly use and prefer over the ones that don't bring me as much utility as often. I don't throw out the dried orange zest just because I'm not using it; I just have it deprioritized compared to black pepper.

Alternatively, I could have all of my spices randomly strewn about my counter. That would be maddening, as every time I wanted a certain spice, I'd have to look through each and every single one. Or I could organize it by alphabet, region of the world it comes from, or more, but that doesn't mean I'm going to find it easily when I need it.

When we talk about prioritization, we have to come to the hard reality that *some relationships are more important to us than others*. I know, unless you are a true sociopath, it's really uncomfortable to put a value on a person, and then say whether knowing one person is more or less valuable to us than another. But we must.

When we *prioritize*, we are structuring our database around who is more or less likely to impact the goal we set out to achieve. That is different but not completely independent of *organization*, in which we are trying to bring structure to an otherwise chaotic and random mess.

Functionally, our database is indifferent to how we approach prioritization, putting the onus on us. The CRM contains different categories or groupings of information, just like the folders on your desktop. The tools, while they may advise and suggest, rely on us as the ultimate arbiter, so we must prescribe for the system the structure we want to follow.

Let's look at examples of organization so we can understand the differences.

Organized Database

- Leads
- Past clients
- People in Washington, DC
- CEOs
- Investors

Now, what if we were to prioritize instead?

Prioritized Database

- Hot leads
- Cold leads
- Top past clients
- Potential mentors
- Current investors
- Prospective investors

Hopefully, the difference is starting to emerge. In the first list, I've organized relationships logically—can't argue when someone in my database lives in New York, or bears the title CEO, or is someone I've transacted with in the past. If you were to ask me who is more important to me using this strategy, however, I wouldn't know. No one would.

Now let's look at the prioritized list. It's clear that I should be spending more time staying engaged with my hot leads as they are much more likely to work with me than my cold leads. If I had 1,000 past clients, maybe my top past clients are the 100 that I'd love to work with again, or I know are well connected for a referral. Depending on whether or not I'm raising money, I could be spending more time courting a partnership with a new investor, or just keeping our current investors abreast of our progress.

Prioritization over Organization
Lets Us Focus on Our Goals

If we organize instead of prioritizing, when it comes to identifying who we should be spending our time building a deeper relationship with, we'll be at a loss. Or worse, we will misallocate our time.

Just to be clear, I'm not saying that you *shouldn't* organize. It is very helpful to identify in your database, for example, the city of most of your contacts, so that you can quickly zoom in on people in a certain city you're traveling to. But if all you have is organization, you're making it nearly impossible to identify which people you care *more* about meeting with when visiting a particular city.

REVISITING PRIORITIZATION

Let's dig in a bit deeper and determine the prioritization of relationships.

You may rank by:

- Recency of last transaction

- Likelihood of opportunity

- Value of opportunity

- Status or prominence

- Response rate

There is no right or wrong answer. Nor will choosing one over another doom you to going out of business.

Prioritization allows you to quickly identify where to spend your time. This is the ultimate goal and lesson of this chapter. How do we identify who we spend our work hours with?

Here is a simple exercise! Try splitting each of the buckets you've created in two. For example, one of my top goals with my relationships is to hire great talent. I have a bucket of prospective employees, and I have a bucket of top hires. The top hires are the dream executives, designers, and developers I want to work with one day. I follow the 80/20 rule here. I keep the top 20 percent in the top hires bucket. When we're dividing our buckets, we're identifying the layers within them, ensuring we spend more time on relationships of higher potential value.

On a normal day, I make sure to talk to those people first, and those are the ones I may spend a lot more time delivering value to.

Addition by Subtraction

The fewer people we focus on, the more time we can focus on those people.

If I were to look at my e-mail account, contact list, and pick-your-favorite social media account, I would probably find upward of 3,000 people whom I have, at some point, interacted with. Are they all important? Yes, you say? OK, great. Let's say that I want to stay in touch with all of them every 30 days. That means I now have to engage with 100 people a day. And respond to their responses, and those responses. If you knew that sitting down for a 30-minute coffee meeting once a year was your best way to build a relationship, that's 3,000 cups of coffee a year. Hopefully, your barista will ask you if having 8.2 cups every day is safe.

It's estimated that we'll meet around 10,000 people in our lifetime. At any point, we'll likely only be able to recall around 150 (Dunbar's number), so how many *should* we be engaging with?

Well, we should be engaging with however many are above a certain threshold of importance. Don't worry, we're not saying that anyone below that threshold is dead to you and you should never respond to their e-mail. But when it comes to who you should spend your time trying to engage with, you need to focus on the top X percent. You can still have a full database of everyone you know, and you can rely on software to keep tabs on them.

The tighter your prioritization, the more focused you are on the people who have the opportunity to make the most impact on your career, the easier the wheel of relationship marketing can turn. Getting this right is foundational to making the next steps in the CAPITAL strategy easier or harder, as we will be able to easily determine who to add value to without much concern about the validity of that person to the level of effort we're going to be investing.

When choosing who to prioritize, it's important to consider two aspects of their importance: one, their general level of perceived value to us, regardless of time horizon or the presence of an opportunity, and two, when there is an active issue on which to engage with them.

Don't Think Binary—It's Tiers

When we talk about prioritization, it's not simply about asking, "Are they important or not?" There's a lot of gray area in between.

When we talk about prioritization, we are looking to determine the importance of one relationship *relative to* others.

Let's take three people:

- Bob, came in as an Internet lead two months ago, was looking for a $250,000 starter home, you haven't spoken since.

- Nancy, member of the PTA, you sold a $750,000 home to her four years ago.

- Sarah, your 15-year old niece who swears Taylor Swift is her spirit animal.

Clearly, you are going to spend more time building a relationship with Nancy, who could provide you with great referrals and may be in the market for something new in the next few years. And while you want to maintain your relationship with your niece, you might not devote your precious weekday hours to engaging.

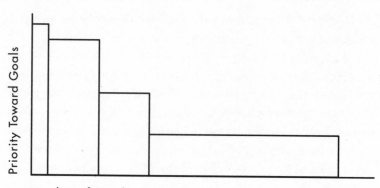

Prioritize based on buckets.

It's nearly impossible to try to stack-rank all of our relationships one by one—that's a recipe for disaster. Going through the previous sorting exercise with thousands of contacts, and more coming in every day, can reduce even the most productive of us to a withering mess.

Rather than relationship-by-relationship ranking, our strategy centers on constructing concentrated lists of contacts of similar priority and goal, and then prioritizing based on those. This does, however, compel the need to be selective about those buckets, lest we create too many and overwhelm ourselves. Determining the right resolution is important, as too many groupings adds greater complexity and potentially slows us down.

Too many buckets:

- Top 5 past clients

- Top 20 past clients

- Top 30 past clients

- ...

Too few buckets:

- Past clients

- Current clients

Just right:

- Top past clients

- Top current clients

- Past clients

- Current clients

This allows us to invest more time more often with our higher-priority relationships and less time less often with our lower-tier relationships.

CHARLES BLACK, AGENT AND LUXURY DIRECTOR OF COMPASS

Hollywood is a hypercompetitive, cutthroat world where everyone is trying to stand apart from the crowd and get ahead in the residential real estate market. Charles Black knows it well.

It's commonly said, "You are the average of the five people you most associate with." I apply that thinking to ensure that I'm focusing on the people who themselves are surrounded by high net worth individuals. From a luxury real estate perspective, this means bucketing your contacts according to net worth. We will have a much greater chance of getting a high dollar referral from someone in this bucket as opposed to someone whose five associates make an average salary. We definitely believe in tiering our relationships, which means we separate out people who have sent multiple referrals, people who have sent one or two, or people who *would* send if they had a better relationship with me. That ensures I'm focusing the right amount of effort on the right relationships.

The uncomfortable feeling we get from ranking people may remind us of our earlier point regarding seeking personal gain from our sphere of influence. We're not saying that someone is more or less important than the other. It's about how pertinent they are to what you are trying to accomplish. Try doing a quarterly phone call with your entire database. Or worse yet, a random assortment of them. How long can that last?

BEING MINDFUL OF STAGE

We've just talked about identifying people we should engage with based on how their position or role relates to what you are trying to achieve long term. We also have to be aware that our relationship management objectives may differ based on the stage in a relationship we're at with someone.

For example, if a buyer is at the end of a sales process, it may not be necessary to consider this person someone you need to engage with. However, if someone is actively in the process of making a buying decision, that is a person you have to prioritize above all else.

You may quickly jump to the conclusion that what we're talking about here is the classic sales funnel (leads, prospects, and customers), which, yes, is the most common solution. But before we think solely in terms of "how many hoops do I have to jump through before they sign on the dotted line" and you go bang that celebratory gong, we shouldn't limit ourselves solely to the end of a transaction. We should be thinking about any type of sequence with multiple stages that are linked together, not necessarily bound to the beginning or end of a transaction.

- Interest, Presale, Sale, Active Client, Past Client

- Accepted Offer, Due Diligence, Ready to Close, Closing, Closed

Prioritizing people by sequence roots back into the overarching goals you're looking to achieve, the types of people that can best contribute to those goals, *and the situations you may find yourself in with them.*

When you first meet someone you identify as potentially valuable, there may be a *ramp-up* or *evaluation* phase. There could be an initial stage where you are kicking off a productive relationship ("well begun is half done"). You may also decide to capture everyone you meet, and at a later point make the call to their level of prioritization.

DID SOMETHING JUST HAPPEN?

Our relationships have a level of perceived value associated with them, and the stage at which they may be does not have to conflict with that. In this situation, we want to anchor our sequence around a particular inciting event.

Here are some examples to think about:

- People who have just completed a transaction with you.

- People who have just expressed interest in your services.

- New referrals.

- People you've otherwise just met.

- Someone you're trying to hire.

- Someone you've *just* hired.

It can also get into the more personal:

- People who have just changed jobs.

- People who have just gotten married, divorced, or expanded their family.

You may immediately think that most of these warrant a discrete action based on these inciting incidents. But by properly capturing the point-in-time stage of the relationship, one can leverage those immediately or later on to build deeper authenticity. Just as we naturally recall that a longtime friend was recently married and keep that in mind whenever interacting with them, a professional associate we care about as well should be given the same treatment.

While most people *still* don't do it, it's generally proper to send a "nice meeting you" e-mail shortly after meeting someone at an event, likely accompanying a connection request on the current flavor-of-the-month social network. But if you were to very easily capture *all* the people you meet in one place, you can go deeper than that. Hypothetically you can go back and review those people at different intervals to determine what next steps you should go through with them. You could also plan to take certain actions with them over a period of time as the relationship progresses, or even automate it. We'll tackle this further when we talk about adding value and timing.

FILL THE BUCKETS

OK, so you have the overall structure for your sphere. That scaffolding is so powerful for you, and it will do wonders. But for now, you must fill it.

There really is no magic formula. This is reliant on *you* identifying the right people with whom your relationship achieves one of the priorities you set.

At Contactually, our team has invested a lot of time and sweat into identifying—more technically, *predicting*—which relationships are important to you, and how. We can also do some base predictions: *who is business relevant?* As much as technology can aid us in many areas of our lives, you, as the manager of the asset, need to be the ultimate arbiter of who is important to you, how, and how much.

As you're ramping up, know that this will be an up-front time investment. That's why the structure that you create, in whatever database or system you choose to use, *needs* to be able to go with you. You should be able to export your assembled knowledge and resurrect it in any system. This further emphasizes the need to, when choosing your tools, identify your ownership of the data and evaluate the ease with which you can take it with you.

KEEP IT UPDATED

Whenever we recall a contact in our database or receive a task or notification about a contact, it should trigger the question, "Is this relationship important to my current goals?" If you don't have a positive response to that question, then this should be a sign that you don't have your relationships prioritized—or at least, it's not reflective of your current business and priorities.

Constantly buying and selling in the stock market is a bit extreme when it comes to financial management. No reasonable head of household would be expected to review their portfolio and make changes every day. But periodic reevaluation of your monetary assets is healthy, leading you to rebalance your investment allocation based on your level of risk, current savings goals, and the realities of the market.

The same goes here. Regular maintenance and tuning of your relationship capital assets should be done, whereas constantly second-guessing yourself is unproductive.

We recommend that it's worth reevaluating your network setup at least once a quarter. Do your buckets still represent the goals you are trying to achieve? Do your contacts still represent what you are hoping to accomplish with their help? It will come as no surprise that the importance of certain contacts may have shifted over time. As you're reviewing your sphere, don't be surprised if you find yourself practicing addition via subtraction, removing more contacts than you add.

Not only do relationships change in priority, but the entire structure of your database may shift as well.

When I was running a consulting firm, I was fortunate to be surrounded by amazing talent looking for jobs all the time. But I wasn't hiring. I was pretty strict that I wanted to keep it a one-person shop, with a bevy of contractors so that I could scale up or down as needed. I didn't care about keeping track of potential hires.

When I started Contactually, hiring became one of my most critical tasks as CEO. Tracking relationships with talented people became incredibly important.

Now that Contactually is well staffed and I have a team solely focused on recruiting, keeping track of hires isn't as important anymore. Now, what's important is maintaining excellent relationships with investors we may want to partner with one day, and staying in touch with the executives at most of our larger enterprise customers.

If I had kept my database structured the same way in 2018 as it was in 2011, my sphere of influence would not be reflective of my current priorities.

As part of your maintenance ritual, ask yourself:

- Is the structure of my database prioritized appropriately, reflective of my current and longer-term objectives?

- Are the people in my buckets reflective of their current or future importance to my goals?

GETTING TACTICAL

With most of our relationships in one place, we should now be able to get into the hard work of prioritizing them. If you need a refresher on how to build your personal database, and the importance of such, revisit the previous chapter on Aggregation.

Setting Up

- Reflect on what the big goals are that you're seeking help with from your sphere.

- Brainstorm the types of people that are *most likely* able to help you achieve each of those goals.

- For each of those types of relationships, identify specific buckets of people in your network that have a likelihood of delivering value.

- If appropriate, tier out relationships based on their relative importance or priority, putting fewer people at the highest priority levels.

As You Are Meeting and Engaging with New People

- If they fit into one of your buckets, add them.

Weekly or Monthly

- Look at people you've been engaging with recently and add them to a bucket.

- Revisit the people in each of these buckets. Do they still belong there?

Quarterly or Annually

- Revisit your goals. Do they still reflect what you believe is most important to you long term?

- Adjust the types of buckets you have as needed. You can keep the bucket to maintain that grouping of people, but you may need to deprioritize.

QUICK WIN

Identify five types of people that will help you with your main goal for the year, and pick 50 people that fall into those five types.

KEY TAKEAWAYS

- Prioritizing your relationships around your ultimate goals will ensure that you are focusing on the right people.

- Prioritize, don't organize.

- Prioritization may also depend on the particular stage of a relationship relative to your ultimate goal with that person.

- Periodic adjusting of your database, buckets, and contacts ensures your sphere is always set up to help you achieve your goals.

CHAPTER

8

INVESTIGATE: COLLECTING INTELLIGENCE ON THE PEOPLE WHO ARE MOST IMPORTANT TO YOU

People do business with people they know.

What does it mean to *know* each other? Think about a colleague, partner, or vendor with whom you feel you have a good relationship. What does that normally entail?

- A track record of (at least mostly) positive interactions

- Personal information about them, plus them having personal information about you

The former is 100 percent in your control. As for the latter, the best tool you have to *amplify your relationship* is to show that you know the individual you have a relationship with. That's what we're talking about when it comes to intelligence.

Think back to our people, processes, and systems combination, we're going to apply that here. First, we're going to focus on the *what* and *how* of capturing as much relationship intelligence as possible, both through the practice of insanely good note-taking (process) and having a strong center of intelligence (systems). Once we feel we have those on lock, we'll go over how to effectively research online to pull up as much information as possible about our relationships. Then—and this is what I find the most effective—we'll dive into how to make the most of our one-on-one interactions. This will include one of my favorite challenge points: the value of supposedly "worthless" small talk.

Seriously, small talk. You would be amazed how the personal information you have about a contact, when properly captured and deployed, can open doors for you.

SMALL BITS MATTER

Let's talk about Stephen.

Stephen had the potential to be the perfect hire for us—or at least, would know the perfect hire. Having no connections to him, I cold e-mailed him and asked if he would be willing to meet. To my surprise, he said he would give me some time if I would come out to meet him, a 45-minute drive away. I'll spare you the details of the conversation, but we wrapped up our meeting with a plan to "keep in touch." As we were making our way out of the coffee shop, I casually inquired about his weekend plans because it was a Friday. He mentioned he was going to a free-throw tournament, as his son was a strong basketball player.

Normally that kind of information from small talk would be "dropped on the floor" and forgotten. However, as I was working on my notes immediately after the meeting, I jotted down that detail, "Stephen's son loves basketball, playing in a free-throw contest."

When I returned to the office, I started to write a thank you e-mail. But upon reviewing my notes, I closed the editor, went to Amazon, and sent him a new basketball, along with a personal note.

The next week, an e-mail arrived:

> Hi Zvi—thanks very much for the basketball. My son uses it every day. So if he wins, you deserve all the credit since he's been using that ball to practice :-)
>
> Separately, meet [his contact] here in the NOVA area. I've known him for more than 12 years and he is a very accomplished and well respected marketing executive with an impressive background in some of the most successful technology companies in the area.

Executive recruiters' fees land in the five-to-six-figure range to get the right people in front of you. I was able to connect with an amazing candidate because of small talk, good note-taking, and $10 worth of rubber. To this day, Stephen is still a valuable person in my sphere, as I am in his.

If I were to pay $10 for his coffee, Stephen would see it as a nice gesture. But by buying the basketball, I demonstrated that I know Stephen and I have a personal relationship with him already. My desire to help him by buying his kid a basketball appeared extremely thoughtful and was valuable to him. This is the goal: to demonstrate thoughtfulness, even in business relationships.

The one bit of intelligence it took to create this moment was a passing mention of his weekend activities. The only effort it took was a few seconds to note that in my database.

Think about my interaction with Stephen.

Core information:

- His general bio because it was an introductory meeting

- What he is looking for, if anything

- Whether he is a fit for my needs

- Verbalized next steps

Metadata:

- Where and when we met

- What he eats or how he dresses if it's remarkable in any way

- Any common connections that came up in the conversation

- Attitude toward me

- His level of interest in any of the topics that came up

- How miserably cold it was when we met

- What his weekend plans were

- Family structure

I could have focused only on tracking and recording the core information. To be clear, writing just those facts down would be better than what most people do, which is nothing. But it's the metadata about our interaction that was the distinguishing factor between a *contact* and a *relationship*. Much of my encounter with Stephen was already recorded; the calendar event knows when and where we met, for example. The rest just took a bit more effort. As we see from the story, that is what makes the difference. That's the value of *intelligence*.

INTELLIGENCE: THE METADATA OF ENGAGEMENT

In software, we often talk about metadata, the seemingly inconsequential information that surrounds the main content. Take an e-mail for example. We naturally focus on the core substance of the message: the text that the other person wrote to us, plus any attachments. However, there is a massive wealth of metadata surrounding each message that you may never see unless you look for it: the e-mail client that was used, the time the message was sent, what servers it bounced through around the world before arriving in your mailbox, where it was sent from, who else was included on the message. Beyond that, even more information can be generated by clicking on the message. When it was opened, how many times it was opened, where it was opened from, what e-mail client the viewer was using, and what computer or phone the person has.

If that seems scary to you, snap out of it. That information is there. What matters is, can you capitalize on it? I'll give you an example.

One of the key ideas behind our software is that metadata can be super helpful to the end recipient. If the metadata in our e-mail can tell us who we've been contacting and when, and who responded or opened a message and when, we can start to deduce key insights about our networks.

That's the kind of information that I want you to value when you are thinking about your sphere of influence.

Without a doubt, ensuring you are capturing the core of your interactions matters—notes about their needs, clear next steps—but when we move beyond the obvious, there is tremendous opportunity.

Systematizing Your Intelligence Collection

We're exposed to an immense amount of information on a daily basis in every action or interaction, and most of it is completely forgotten.

Remember the administrator at my university with the uncanny ability to remember the most insignificant details about people? He's blessed with the amazing gift of memory. Me? I can barely remember who I met yesterday.

We mere mortals have to rely on technology to collect, store, and recall pertinent points about our relationships. This enables us to break through the barrier of "just another business card."

Luckily, gathering intelligence is pretty easy if we systematize it. It starts with the realization that you must have a centralized place to collect, organize, and review your intelligence.

Systems to Consider

The tool you use should be easy to operate, be able to store many notes about people, and be accessible anywhere. I urge you to find whatever is best for you. Here are examples of what other people have used:

- **A simple spreadsheet.** You may quickly record notes on napkins or pieces of paper, but at the end of the day, transfer these to a sheet. Each row is a contact, and you have multiple columns for different identifying pieces of information.

- **Your contact manager or CRM.** There is only one static "notes" field for each contact, but you can easily append pieces of information.

- **A specific note-keeping tool.** I use Contactually for storing notes about people, but I use Evernote right now as a repository for pretty much any other note or thought. Synced between all devices, you can have one file on every contact and keep a running dossier of every other note and to-do.

- **A notebook.** For some, paper still wins. Have half a page or a page dedicated to each relationship, and you can flip through to find the person and record a quick note.

Understand What You're Looking for: Social Objects

Social object theory purports that social interactions revolve around a certain object, event, or idea.

When two people meet for dinner, the dinner is the social object. When they discuss last week's game at the table, the game is the social object. And when they see a movie afterward, the social object is—you guessed it—the movie.

These social objects aren't necessarily the reason two people get together. If people interact in a different setting, they will likely interact around other social objects, such as common interests or ideologies. There is always a catalyst for interaction, and that something is the social object.[1]

To some extent, any personal detail you've garnered about a person is a social object between the two of you. It demonstrates a shared connection.

But what's much better are the social objects that you *generate together* or *already have together*.

There are many planes on which social objects can exist. The obvious ones are schools, fields of study, ethnic backgrounds, hometowns, and membership in fraternities or sororities. If you find information that becomes a valuable social object via research or interaction, it's worth noting right from the start. And don't forget that the interaction itself is, or can be, a social object.

What's important is that you get into the practice of recording notes. In case it hasn't yet become apparent, ensuring you capture as much information as possible is critical. Our intelligence efforts have the ability to unearth a tremendous amount of information. As valuable as that can be in aggregate, it is inconsequential unless we write it down.

As we discussed in Chapter 2, our memory decays. We may have walked out of that coffee shop with clear-as-day knowledge, including next steps, personal details about a contact's family, and the ridiculously large muffin she ordered. Because we see it so clearly now, the need to record it doesn't seem so pressing.

Pinch yourself. Hard.

You absolutely need to record this.

There is no right or wrong answer as to how or where you structure your notes as long as you are able to retrieve and understand them.

For example:

- As you're discovering information, look for key attributes like "Enjoys basketball," "Needs hot sauce on everything," "Wife is named Becky."

- As soon as possible after (or during) a meeting or research session, record these notes. Remember, the notes will be used by you or people close to you, so they can be as raw and honest as possible.

- Make it an end-of-day, even end-of-meeting ritual to record anything you've discovered in your interactions.

- Recording information is only useful if you actually consume it. When you are meeting with someone, establish a practice of looking at your previous notes.

- Keep at it!

How do you record information when you're at an event or interacting with a lot of different people at once? Through one of our partners, we've gotten to know one of the best software trainers in the real estate industry, Lance Pendleton. We asked him to share some of his best practices. He simply said . . .

Have a small bladder.

OK, we're going to need to explain that.

When you are interacting with a lot of people, whether at a networking event, conference, or party, you'll have many sequential interactions. Each of them generates much of the aforementioned information that can be incredibly helpful when it comes to building a relationship. However, as we all know, too often that information or the relationship itself is whittled down to one in a stack of dog-eared business cards that you fish out of your pocket as you're about to throw those pants in the wash.

Lance's solution is simple and elegant. After every interaction, excuse yourself to go to the bathroom. Stand in the hallway (or bathroom) and record everything you just spoke about with this person. Then head back to the event. It may take you another few minutes per conversation, but recording that information for later processing can vastly increase the likelihood that your interaction turns into a real connection.

Another simple tactic is to record next steps right on their business card. Unless they have one of those glossy business cards that you can't write on. (Savages.)

Taking Structured Notes

I'm the guy who is always lugging around my laptop, power cord, battery backup, tablet computer, phone, cords, and anything else I might need in case of a presentation or emergency. But when I'm networking or at a conference, I rely on my iPad. I bring it to every meeting. To avoid being rude or distracted, I always start off by asking, "Is it OK if I take notes? I want to ensure this is valuable for both of us." *Saying that alone* adds value to the relationship because it shows that I care enough about this interaction to guarantee there will be next steps, and I'm not going to forget anything we spoke about.

In some cases, getting out my iPad may not be appropriate. For example, we have a *no device* policy for most meetings at Contactually to ensure none of us gets distracted. In that case, a notepad is a transparent way of showing you're focused while capturing notes.

Bringing a consistent structure to your notes can aid the relationship further than general note-taking. Consistent structure ensures that you are collecting the right information from each interaction and can help train your mind to gain this intelligence with every conversation.

Furthermore, when it comes to recalling those notes, you'll be able to quickly scan through particular sections to gain exactly what you need to know. Checking multiple notes allows you to start seeing a trend.

USING THE WEB FOR RECONNAISSANCE

Here are a few best practices for conducting online research. Generally, these tactics take only five minutes per contact.

- Start by looking for the obvious. What social media profiles or web links do you already have? These could be in your CRM, in their e-mail signature, or on their business card. People are much more comfortable sharing personal profiles these days, so don't be afraid to click through them.

- Do a quick web search for the person's name. If your search brings up information for other people with the same name (luckily the name Zvi Band is pretty unique!), try including their city. Search for "John Sorbet Washington DC."

- Pull up their profile on LinkedIn, and see what you can find about recent job changes, personal interests, non-profit boards, etc.

- As you look through every profile and search result, try to pull together relevant facts that can be used in future activities. What they do today may not be that interesting, but what they do outside of work, the trajectory of their career, what they post about—*that* is interesting.

Start making notes *before* the meeting or phone call, and use them to record any interesting research.

A web search is table stakes, the basic work that any professional should be doing. Spend enough time so you don't walk into a meeting with no idea what to talk about.

CHRIS FRALIC, PARTNER AT FIRST ROUND CAPITAL

Well before starting Contactually, I had the opportunity to get to know Chris Fralic. Chris has helped foster companies to be the household brands we know today. While venture capital is an increasingly commoditized industry as more money comes in, Chris and his team remain among the most sought-after investors in part, as Chris says, because "connecting with people has always been my core competency—in business and in life—and I love that my work lets me blend the two."

If you're able to do real research about the other person before a meeting, it stands out. Often I'll have entrepreneurs come and pitch, and there's no evidence that they've done much research on us besides knowing that we have money. I think it's a fairly low bar that most people don't take the time to cross.

I think, at a simple level, reviewing your past e-mails can provide clues. Look through your e-mail threads to see, "What has been discussed previously? What communication outreach response has happened?" I'm looking for reminders of previous conversations, points brought up, any other threads of conversation that could be helpful. Sometimes I find I wouldn't have remembered them all if I hadn't gone back in and looked for them.

Go on to people's Twitter account or their LinkedIn or other social media, and see what they've published. Are they talking about anything? Are they retweeting or engaging in some subject or with someone? That's an interesting thing to know. Did they write an article that might be relevant? Being aware of that stuff is a good place to start. It could be a good point of connection about something that they recently wrote or talked about that might be interesting to you, even if you disagree with it.

The thing you want to gain is familiarity in my mind, that's all. You want to be careful not to make it creepy or stalky. We shouldn't pretend we know everything about each other. It's not appropriate for me to ask about your kids by name when I've never met them. I think that's taking it too far, but it isn't uncommon that for some reason both of you are connected to someone else in the social media, and you can get a glance. Sometimes in that regard, I'll say to people, "It looks like you're having a great summer from all the pictures on Facebook." To me, that's an appropriate way of acknowledging it without diving too deeply into it.

GAINING INTELLIGENCE VIA INTERACTIONS

When we think about our friends and family, we know everything about them. Their spouse's name, their past relationships, their irrational fear of latex balloons. So if we know so much about our friends but so little about our professional connections, and people do business with people they know, how can we get to know more about our professional contacts?

With friends, we have the luxury of years of casual, trivial conversations. We don't have the defensive barriers, facades, and ulterior motives that come into play in a professional context. When it comes to relationship building, the key is to gain and record key points that show you care about these contacts.

Whenever you can, try to meet people face-to-face. We tend to hide behind our social media feeds and e-mail. We often don't feel comfortable or see the value in face-to-face meetings. I *love* meeting people! As introverted as you may be, this is one of the most powerful methods you have to build rapport and create social objects. Yes, it may take more time, but it is exponentially more meaningful.

On the days when I have 10 or 12 calls, I may not be able to easily recall any of my conversations. But the face-to-face meetings I have stick out in my memory. It's not a voice on the phone; it's a human. Our goal is to break down the barrier between the professional facade and the real human being behind it. If you aren't able to meet for a quick 20-minute coffee or afternoon frozen yogurt, then do a face-to-face video conference call.

The Output of Every Interaction: The Four Points of Information to Collect

Whether it's your first interaction or your fifteenth, here are the four points of information to gather when you meet with your contacts.

- **Current state of your relationship.** Are they friendly? Do they have any interest in you? What is your personal

opinion of the interaction? How would you rate or prioritize them?

- **Current state of their business.** This is where you'll record
  the main meat of what you learned in the conversation,
  and it's usually about their trade. What are their goals for
  the year? What is the biggest challenge they are currently
  facing? What are they most proud of right now? What do
  they value? What can you thank them for?

- **Next steps from an interaction.** Make sure to capture not
  only business tasks but other personal tasks. For example,
  send them a book that you mentioned or a funny article
  that came to mind.

- **Personal details.** Write down any intelligence you've
  collected on them, no matter how minor. Record any common social objects. "Also went to Maryland, also thinks
  coffee is a socialist conspiracy."

If you're still an analog fan, open up your favorite notepad and
divide a page into four sections. After a meeting (or before, if you
are able to prepare in advance), record these four bullet points in
your database or other note-taking app.

Remember, without being too aggressive, you want to be able
to garner helpful information that you can use at a future time.

Acting on the Next Steps

The foundation of a good interaction is actually doing what you say
you are going to do. This sounds basic, but I cannot stress enough
how important this is. The prominent venture capitalist Chris
Fralic, who is known as a super-connector in technology circles,
argues that "actually doing what you say you're going to do will put
you in the top quartile."[2]

Just because your list of commitments is clear as day now does
not mean it will remain so. Instantly recording what's on your to-
do list during or immediately after your meeting is an important
habit to cultivate.

The Gold Mine of Personal Details and Off-the-Record Information

We're illogical humans, not robots. When we're interacting one-on-one, it's rude (if not entirely *impossible*) to have a conversation that is 100 percent centered on the sole objective. If it were, we would just send document edits, questions, and tasks back and forth without relating to one another. Our minds would go numb.

When we're interacting, there is so much more going on in our communication, both spoken and unspoken. Whether it's direct or reading-between-the-lines, so much personal and professional information is revealed.

Why? People love talking about themselves.

In his perennial classic *How to Win Friends and Influence People*, Dale Carnegie wrote, "Talk to people about themselves, and they will listen for hours."

But you actually have to care.

Here's the trick: don't do this unless you *genuinely* care about the person. If you authentically, personally value the person you're engaging with, lean into that. You're not prying when asking questions. This is why we selectively choose to engage with only the people we've prioritized.

On the business side, asking, "How's [insert company, nonprofit, or cult] going?" can open up a conversation. That question should only be the opening volley; you'll likely get the press release. Capture their answer, but you can assume that you're not getting the full story. Be ready to dig deeper.

Let's be clear: While there is a good chance you are interested in the organization someone works for, you care more about how *the person* is doing. So follow up by asking how *they* are doing in light of whatever company news they shared. That's where you can identify clues to understand more. This can result in a deeper understanding of the person and the state of their business.

Ask:

- **How business is going.** Unless you are already close, expect a PR-approved answer, involving the words "busy" or "crushing it."

- **How they are doing in the business.** You'll shift the conversation to be much more focused on them, which can be a 180-degree difference from the previous question.

- **About their current challenges.** Hopefully, they'll have a clear idea of what those are and what they need from the universe (you) to resolve them.

- **What's next.** This is generic enough that you might be surprised with the results, so keep the aperture open here. If they are secure and stable, they might be focused on where the business is taking them. If they are "making moves," they'll mention it. You would be shocked how many times I've asked that question only to learn that my associate is job searching.

Don't forget the personal side. To get you off the ground, here are some tactics that can help naturally bring out who they really are:

- Ask them what made them become [whatever their profession is]. Rarely are people forced into a career against their will, so there must have been a reason or chain of events that brought them to where they are now.

- Ask them what brought them to live [wherever they are living]. They usually have a story. Except people from Texas. If you're born in Texas, you will usually die in Texas. I can't explain that.

- If your conversation bookends a weekend or holiday, ask about their plans. You can gain a lot of intelligence by seeing what people do outside of their nine-to-five.

- If you gain some tidbits about their family, dive into that, too. What does their spouse do? What are their kids obsessed with these days? What are their summer plans?

The Value of Good Small Talk

As I've alluded to a number of times so far, conversation unrelated to the primary topic is a gold mine when you're trying to build a relationship. This "small talk" is often incredibly relevant.

Small talk is often dismissed as empty conversation about the weather and other mundane subjects, meaningless preamble to ease into a discussion. Some abhor it and prefer to dive right into the deep stuff. But used correctly, it can foster trust, understanding, and a genuine sense of reciprocity between two people.

Northwestern University law professor Janice Nadler conducted an experiment in which students were paired up and tasked with coming to a business agreement in a week's time. Each pair had conflicting interests that would make negotiations challenging, and they could only discuss business over e-mail. However, prior to negotiations, half the pairs had a phone conversation in which they engaged in small talk and got to know each other.

After the week of negotiations, Nadler found the pairs who engaged in small talk were four times as likely to reach an agreement than those who didn't. Almost across the board, these conversations created a sense of trust, familiarity, and accountability even though they had only spoken once over the phone.

The pairs who jumped right into e-mail had a harder time and were more prone to agitation, suspicion, and gridlocked conflict that brought negotiations to a grinding halt. They behaved competitively and made threats to walk away from the deal.[3]

Even if you can't meet customers face-to-face, it's vital you establish rapport with them. The most trivial small talk over the phone can lead to the most valuable relationships.

Small talk is relevant here as it can generate a vast amount of knowledge about a contact's family, life, and hobbies. Capturing this information will aid your goals and can help build rapport.

Think about topics that often come up and how you can use those as starting points.

- Talk about traffic or issues getting to the meeting. Ask where they live and for how long.

- Weather? Ask what they like to do in this weather or what their go-to season is.

- Past or upcoming weekend, holiday, or season plans. Don't just accept mundane answers like "watching football." A harmless follow-up question like "what team are you root-ing for?" or "what do you and your family normally do on weekends?" can illuminate their lives.

Don't consider small talk as simply a required necessity to start and end a meeting. It can be critical for relationship building. Its outcome, as with any interaction, is to establish social objects that can be leveraged later on.

Not Getting Anywhere? Lead by Sharing Your Own Information

Not everyone is going to be an open book, and that's OK. It's still possible to retrieve information and share social objects from the most reserved people. You can skip over the normal icebreaker questions (e.g., *How many jelly beans could fit into this room right now?* My editor challenges whether this is a good icebreaker. I urge you to open your next few conversations with that question.)

A good way to break through the ice wall is to answer the questions yourself. Volunteering information often leads others to reciprocate. It's not foolproof, but it's an effective Plan B.

> ME: "So what are you and the family up to this weekend?"
> THEM: "Oh, not much, just hanging around."
> ME: "Totally get it!"
> SILENCE.
> ME: "My wife and I are taking our daughter to Power Rangers on Ice this weekend. Not sure whether I should be more excited about the exciting dialogue or the thousands of screaming kids."
> THEM: "Hah, that's great. How old are your kids?"
> ME: "We just have a 15-month-old. How about you?"
> THEM: "Great age. I have a five-year-old and a six-year-old."
> ME: "Nice. They going to Power Rangers, too?"
> THEM: "No, we have a hockey match and a ballet recital."

Boom!

GETTING TACTICAL

- Ensure that your database is set up to automatically pull data from online sources; subscribe to third-party services if necessary.

- Take copious notes and capture as much as possible in your database or another note-taking tool.

- When you're engaging with people, capture as much as possible from your interactions. This includes small talk, which you should lean into to gain personal details.

- Subscribe to online services that will alert you to relevant news and updates.

- Follow your contacts on social media.

- Do your research. Find recent online news, social posts, industry news, articles that interest them, and so on. Review past conversations and notes. Any specific relevant points you uncover, log back into your database. You're looking for personal information, business challenges, current priorities, and social objects you have in common.

QUICK WIN

- The next conversation you have with someone in your sphere, take notes about your interaction, including small talk, and add that to your CRM.

KEY TAKEAWAYS

- Recalling personal details and shared social objects helps tremendously when building a strong professional relationship.

- Online research and small talk can yield valuable information.

- Be a meticulous notetaker, not just next steps but personal details as well.

- Collect four points of information: the state of your relationship, the state of their business, next steps, and personal details.

9

TIMELY ENGAGEMENT: BUILDING A RHYTHM TO YOUR FOLLOW-UP

Jane Rodriguez is sitting in her car, taking a sip of her cappuccino as she's waiting for her next appointment. Her phone, which is notifying her of the latest local sports disappointment, starts vibrating with an incoming call. It's an unknown number, which means it is most likely an automated recording offering to increase her "Google ranking," but it might also be a lead.

"Hi, this is Jane!"

"Hey, Jane! This is Dante. We met at Bill Davis's birthday party a few years ago."

"Yes, of course, I remember you!" *(She doesn't.)*

"Well, I was wondering if you were up for taking a look at my house. My wife just got a new job, and sadly, that has us moving out of town in the next few months."

"Of course! When would be a good time?"

Jane is thinking she won the lottery. To be honest, the chances of that happening are like winning the lottery.

Opportunities almost never come like that, and Jane knows it. Jane has completely forgotten about this person, so she can only assume that Dante has forgotten about her. Dante may simply have an amazing memory, or *something else* made Dante think of her. But for the most part, as more time goes by, the more likely people will forget any details about us or their impression of us, forget us entirely, or meet someone else who has the competitive advantage of simply being a more recent encounter.

How often do you need to stay in touch with someone? Could Jane have ensured that Dante would call if she had spoken to him every year? Sent a card every month? Or would she have risked annoying him, to the point of him blocking her number and auto-filtering her mail to the dumpster if she had been reaching out every week?

The time decay of relationships is caused by our own inability to retain memories indefinitely, so we and the people in our sphere slowly drift away from each other. It happens, but at what pace? What is the half-life of a relationship?

"How often should I follow up?" is the most common question I get on webinars. Sadly, it's one I can't easily answer because there is no right answer. The truth is:

> **There is no definite right or wrong cadence at which to engage with people in your sphere.**

There are so many variables at play, not least of which is how our brains store, recall, and overwrite information. Just think of all the things that could have happened after meeting and connecting with someone:

- You didn't build enough rapport with them to leave a lasting impression.

- They met someone else with whom they clicked.

- A friend highly recommended a competitor.

- They lost your card.

- They. Simply. Forgot.

Relationships can have a half-life. We just don't know when it is. People could still remember you 50 years later. Or they could forget you next week.

Our strategy, therefore, is to maintain that relationship through periodic engagements, at intervals or occasions we control.

Remember, the vast majority of your colleagues aren't doing any follow-up, so any engagement you initiate is better than none at all.

You can engage with someone you've prioritized in your sphere using:

- A regular cadence that you've set, such as reaching out to past clients every 90 days

- An event-driven trigger, such as seeing something they posted online

- An intelligence system or other third party that identifies a target for you

We're going to walk through the first two, ensuring that, if nothing else, you are engaging on a regular basis and associating actions with intrinsic or extrinsic events.

SETTING A CADENCE IS MAINLY ABOUT THEIR PRIORITY

The P in CAPITAL is *Prioritize*. When we're thinking about how often to stay in touch with someone, a key factor is their priority level in our sphere. As a general rule of thumb, we want to be spending more time, more often, with our higher-value relationships.

Would it make sense to stay in touch with your newest clients every six months, but all of your past clients every 30 days?

No. Your current clients are the ones who are actively working with you and have the highest propensity to refer you. Your past clients, while important, are less likely to have anything to work on with you. So *relative to each other*, you would want to be engaging with your current clients more often than with your past clients.

Note that when I'm talking about setting the cadence for a relationship based on priority, I am speaking specifically about applying a rule for a *group of homogenous contacts* (our "buckets" metaphor).

Determining the cadence at the individual level introduces too much inconsistency. That was one key lesson we learned early on. It's easy to determine in the moment if someone is a *Top Past Client* or *Low Priority Web Lead*, but asking you how often to stay in touch with any one person, every single time, can lead to analysis paralysis, throwing up your hands in confusion, and diving deep into a pint of ice cream.

If you're not using a system that is specifically set up to allow you to maintain a regular cadence with a contact, you may have to do so manually, setting tasks for yourself for each contact and adjusting as you engage. I know plenty of people who still update a spreadsheet with each communication point or insist on doing this in Outlook.

If you don't have an intelligent CRM that can handle this, you *could* always set a recurring calendar appointment that will remind you to reach out to someone. Just keep in mind that calendar reminders are not informed by anything else, meaning they will remind you of your task even if you spoke to that contact yesterday. The biggest downside, beyond the amount of lift required, is that you're significantly increasing the chance that you *simply forget* one time, leaving the relationship open to slipping through the cracks entirely.

What Is Too Often or Not Often Enough?

Again, there is no hard or fast rule. However, there are some basic guidelines.

Expected transactional frequency. How often you stay in touch with people should have some correlation to how often they expect to need you. How often are they likely to have a referral opportunity? How often are they buying your service or product? You'll want to ensure that you are at least engaging with them as often as their expected frequency.

Adjust to your target. One of the stumbling blocks people find to getting started with relationship marketing is the fear that their outreach is not desired by the target.

The intention in relationship marketing is to make sure that every interaction you have is *personal, meaningful, and valuable.* If you feel that the cadence at which you're interacting with someone doesn't lend itself to those three, then you should adjust your strategy. Adjust your cadence according to contacts' response rates and interest levels.

Keep in mind your own capacity. If I had figured out how to triple underline those words, I would have. How many people fit into your buckets? If your whole sphere comprises only 30 people, then making sure you talk to all of them at least once a month may be fine. On average, that's about one every day. But as your volume increases, the frequency has to be taken into consideration. Keeping in touch with 3,000 people in your network on a personal level in that same time frame means you have to write 100 very personal e-mails a day! Definitely possible, but a lot more work than you may initially expect. Balance is key.

How many times have you gone through a buffet, sat down, and realized that you got way, way too much food? Just as our eyes are bigger than our stomachs, we must realize that we have a habit of creating more work than we actually have the ability to do in a day. So while we have the right intention when determining how often to engage, and we believe we can do it, we aren't the best at thinking through *how much additional work that will be per day*, the tyranny of the urgent that will come up to suck more time away from us, nor what happens when all those people respond to us!

The Biggest Sand Trap in Relationship Marketing

Take a look at one of your buckets of contacts, and how often you *think* you should be following up with them.

**(# of people you want to engage with) ×
(# of times you need to engage them in a given year) =
# of engagements you need to have, at minimum**

For example, you have one bucket of past clients representing 200 relationships. You tell yourself you want to engage with each one once a quarter, or four times a year. That means you will make 800 touchpoints over the year. Of those, approximately half will respond to you. If you proceed with that plan, you're reaching out to an additional three people a day, on top of your day-to-day work, responding to your recent follow-ups. And that's just *one* of your many buckets.

The prime inhibitor of relationship marketing is simply not having the willpower to do the work. The second is not developing the right structure for yourself in the beginning. And just like an all-you-can-eat buffet, it often is due to your eyes being bigger than your stomach.

When setting cadences for your sphere, make sure you really can do the additional work. The likelihood of you missing an opportunity because you followed up once every two months instead of once a month is minimal, compared to being overwhelmed with too many tasks and dropping the ball altogether.

WHEN AN EVENT HAPPENS

Maintaining a minimum cadence for a relationship is a core foundation of our relationship marketing efforts, if nothing else to ensure that the cadence doesn't drop *so* low that any mindshare has completely disappeared. But that doesn't mean we shouldn't be looking for other opportunities for which we can reach out within that cadence. Events, ours or theirs, can serve as context in the outreach.

Their Events

Your contacts have lives of their own. Given our propensity to share our lives online, it can be easy to find and track this information.

These can fall into one of two groups:

- Recurring dates such as birthdays and anniversaries

- Other special occasions such as a promotion or a new position

To the extent you're comfortable, connecting with your prioritized contacts on social media lets you keep an ear to the ground for noteworthy events.

Life Changes

There may be life changes that are relevant to outreach:

- Birthday

- Wedding anniversary

- Birth of a child, baptism, bar mitzvah, etc.

- Home closing (or other major transaction) anniversary

- A death in the family, injury, divorce, or other personal challenges

These are good times to reach out. Who doesn't love getting wished happy birthday? However, keep in mind that, especially in the case of a birthday, there are many others who are reaching out as well. Being unique or creative (like wishing them a happy almost-birthday the day before) might be useful, so set your database appropriately.

For better or for worse, these life change events may bring a tsunami of social media activity to their doorstep, and you risk being just another droplet of seawater. Fear not. When we talk about adding value in the next chapter, we'll give you very specific and tactical advice on how to ensure that you stand out.

It's also important not just to congratulate them in good times. When we're at our weakest is sometimes when we're at our loneliest and most vulnerable. Show you care by reaching out then.

Relevant News

Their company might have been mentioned in the news. They might have had an article written about them. There might be some major industry trend or government news that materially affects them.

Self-Driven Events

From time to time, an occasion driven by you provides the perfect opportunity for you to reach out.

A Holiday That You Want to Share

The holiday card will never die. Everyone sends a card in December. What if you celebrate another holiday? September 26 is National Pancake Day, Shamu the Whale Day, and National Dumping Day!

An Article That's Relevant to Them

In your own personal browsing, you may come across an article that you find interesting. Who else is this interesting to? What names come up first? You can use a tool (we list some in Appendix B) to capture these articles and share them later on, or you can instantly send a "just thinking of you" e-mail right after you read it. Or you can share it on social media and make sure to mention them in your update.

They Just Pop into Your Head

Sometimes certain people suddenly come to mind. You're eating waffles, and you think how much better Belgian waffles are, which makes you think about your trip to Belgium a few years ago, and then you remember that Bob Smith lived in Belgium as a kid. Bob Smith! How's he doing? Don't be afraid to use that as a trigger to reach out.

Saying Thank You

I was terrible at writing thank you cards as a kid. I think some of my aunts and uncles still harbor ill will toward me because I didn't write them a thank you note for one or another birthday.

Saying thank you is an incredibly powerful tool in your arsenal. It's also something we see very rarely these days—we're so focused on what's next—so being the person who does say thank you can help you stand out. How?

- It completes the loop for people, showing that you received the desired outcome. If you knew that your follow-ups or valuable interactions were fully received, you'd know that it was worth continuing, right?

- It shows that you value what they did, and therefore your relationship.

- It is yet one more opportunity to engage with a particular contact and further build mindshare.

- It makes you—and them—feel better. A 2003 study by Robert Emmons and Michael McCullough[1] showed that those who listed the things they were grateful for had higher life satisfaction. It also feels good to be thanked.

- Say thanks for even the smallest things. I was once speaking on a panel and was handed a handwritten thank you note afterward by one of the attendees. She wrote it as I was speaking! She said that she writes thank you notes for everyone, even a restaurant's wait staff.

GETTING TACTICAL

Let's roll up our sleeves and get down to business. I will remind you, dear reader, that the cadence you set is far less important than actually engaging.

Subscribe to External Events

This is about listening.

- Subscribe to people's updates on whatever social platforms they seem active on.

- Leverage any predictive analytics tools that might be applicable to your industry, including website tracking and big data tools.

- Subscribe to a product that can feed you relevant events, like press mentions or company updates.

Remember Important Dates

- If there are any specific dates or instances to reach out (like an agreed upon catch-up call), set that in whatever system you are using.

- Remember birthdays, personal anniversaries, work anniversaries, kids' ages, etc., and set reminders in your database.

Establish a Catchall Cadence

- Depending on the importance, quantity, and urgency of a type of relationship, put that bucket of contacts on a particular schedule. Using once every 90 days as a baseline, increase the frequency if they are important to you or in an active buying cycle, and decrease the frequency for larger numbers of individuals on longer time horizons.

- Periodically review those rules and adjust them based on your current priorities. If you are extra busy, following up with someone bimonthly instead of monthly will cut your work in half and likely not have a major impact on your results.

QUICK WIN

Take 100 of your most important contacts and set a reminder to follow up with them once a quarter. That's about one additional conversation a day. Every 90 days or four times a year is a good middle ground.

KEY TAKEAWAYS

- While there are no set rules on how often you should engage with the people who matter to you, the key is to set a minimum cadence for a bucket of relationships.

- As you're determining how often to stay in touch, keep in mind the amount of additional work you're creating for yourself, the relative importance of each bucket of contacts, and the frequency of opportunities that these might yield.

- Beyond just staying in touch every so often at a minimum, be on the lookout for other events that provide an opportunity to engage.

- Advanced tools can analyze massive datasets and make unexpected recommendations.

ADD VALUE, PART 1: DOING MEANINGFUL ACTIONS

In the absence of value-based engagement with the key relationships in your sphere, we're lacking significant progress toward our ultimate goal of reaping long-term benefits from the people we know, right? Au contraire! Quite the opposite.

- Having a prioritized, clean, rich database of our sphere is itself an incredible asset.

- We need to gain clarity into who would be the best use of our time and resources to engage with—and when.

Everything has come to this point. You know who you want to talk to. You know it's time.

Oh no, what do I say?

I'm with you, sister. But let's be honest, that's not what you're thinking. It's something more like:

What can I do so they'll value me more?

You're also thinking:

How do I not screw this up?

And it's that last point that can disable us. It's not worth telling you how often we get the pushback "I don't know what to say"—because you've thought that to yourself.

In this chapter we're going to walk you through to the answer, as well as seek counsel and ideas from others I've seen do wonderful things. What you and only you have to decide is whether you are going to take these ideas and put them into action. If you don't, the lost opportunities from *inaction* far outweigh any potential negative impact from pressing that big Send button.

You and your contact are at a key point in your relationship. The vast majority of people will never reengage. The vast majority of connections disappear. The names and faces we once knew, even for a fleeting moment, will fade away. You have every ability to let that happen to this contact. Right now. Maybe by chance some contacts will reach out to you. Or you'll run into each other on the street. Maybe. But probably not. In which case, you are missing out on getting to know them further. On any opportunity they might have provided. Any potential referral or recommendation. Believe it or not, you may be standing at a crucial point in your business, where the only difference is doing something rather than doing nothing.

Hence the opening quote of this chapter. I'm not calling you a coward if you don't press Send. What I am saying is that it is completely OK to be apprehensive. *But then take action.*

> What's the difference between a hero and a coward? There ain't no difference. Inside they're both exactly alike. Both scared of dying or getting hurt. But it's what the hero does that makes him a hero. What the other guy doesn't do that makes him a coward.
> —"CUS" D'AMATO, MIKE TYSON'S TRAINER

Elan and I went to college together. Admittedly, we weren't close, but we were in the same general social circles, at least enough to connect on social media. After graduation, we had both been in start-ups. We connected here and there, did one project together early in our careers, and that was it for a while. I was traveling to Chicago for some meetings, and I knew that he was running marketing for a start-up. The day before my flight, I sent him an e-mail saying I was going to be in town (my trigger) and asked if he wanted to meet up for a quick chat. He obliged, and I swung by his office just to say hi. We hadn't spoken in years, but we still had enough of a connection that it wasn't a completely cold interaction. A few months later, we did the same thing when he came to DC. I mentioned a couple of key hires we had been searching for, and he made one of the best possible introductions ever: the perfect candidate whom I otherwise would never have known. If I hadn't sent Elan that short e-mail while I was packing, my business would never have been the same.

All the advice and knowledge in the world is useless if it is never put into action.

I completely understand the fearful attitude that may prevent us from stepping out of our comfort zones and engaging with someone who we may not know so well (yet). You don't want to be seen as the desperate pest "just following up."

I get it, and that's why I don't want you to follow up. I want you to *add value*.

IT'S NOT ABOUT STAYING IN TOUCH—IT'S ABOUT BEING OF VALUE

A common question we get is about what to say. The assumption is that the way we're going to engage is just to talk to the intended recipient. Let's take a step back and remember the whole hypothesis. People do business with people they know—or alternatively, people they find valuable (knowing someone or having a relationship is valuable in itself). Therefore, when following up, our simple aim is to increase the value of their relationship with us. How does one go about doing that?

Deliver value.

That's a totally different way of thinking about it in the context of relationship marketing. Yes, more often than not the result may be some written or verbal communication to them. But what matters at the core is, are we delivering value, and therefore showing our value to them?

At every point, we should be thinking about delivering value. There are three mindsets when engaging with our sphere, each one laying a very different foundation for how you deliver value.

- The *direct* mindset, in which it's purely your relationship with them on display

- The *community* mindset, in which your way of adding value is introducing them to others

- The *broadcast* mindset, in which you try to engage people on a larger scale, while still maintaining intimacy

There is a vast gap between contacting someone and skipping the relationship entirely. You will do wonders even with just a quick "hi" in a text message. But we are not trying to just get people to recall who we are.

- We want people to think of us at the right opportunity.

- We may be seeking a deeper relationship with that person.

- We would like a continuing connection with that person, which may not be a given.

- We have a specific request or want to be able to make an ask later on.

To be eligible for any of the above, we have to think about being of value to people. The value we provide to others increases the mindshare we have with them.

As time goes on, the amount of mindshare we have decreases. There's a minimum threshold of mindshare, which we want to be above, depending on what we want from our relationships. It depends on the person and the request, so there is no tried and true measure. The perceived value of relationships is also relevant when it comes to the level of lift one might ask of them in the future.

- Hopefully, anyone you know would be willing to say hi to you on the street.

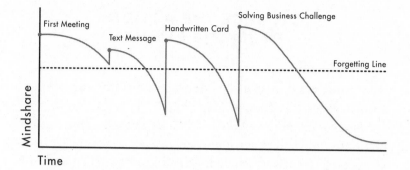

Adding value maintains a relationship and increases your mindshare.

- But expecting them to think of you the next time they need a service you offer requires much more.

- As does asking them to stake their reputation by making an introduction between you and someone else.

Another key way to frame the question is to address it with an elevated level of empathy. How do we want our contact to *feel* when they first receive whatever we've sent them?

- Do we want them to feel appreciative of our relationship?

- Should they immediately call us?

- Do we want to be seen as an expert in some way?

- Do we want them to feel comfortable pulling the trigger on an action?

- Do we want them to promote whatever we've done with others?

- Do we want this item to be a fixture in their home? In their office?

Theoretically, the more value we deliver, the more mindshare we gain with any contact. A stronger, more valuable relationship takes more time to decay and be forgotten.

DIVORCE THE ACTION
FROM THE RESULT

Isaac Newton's third law of motion states that "for every action, there is an equal and opposite reaction."

Save for minor exceptions of technical deliverability issues or getting caught in the spam filter, our engagement will be received by our target (or at least someone assisting the target). I don't think we as a society fully appreciate how powerful that is, that we can now reach pretty much anyone in the world through *some* means. So if we have confidence in identifying the person we want to engage with and have been incited to engage, then . . .

This is where people really get stuck. As we're formulating the right experience to create for our sphere of influence, our pubescent social anxiety suddenly comes back to haunt us.

- Will they respond?

- What if they hate me?

- Do they know who I am?

- Am I going to look like a desperate joker?

And suddenly, we're walking away from the computer to the freezer to down half a pint of Ben and Jerry's and watch a Netflix romantic comedy. Oh, just me? Never mind.

JAYSON GAIGNARD, FOUNDER OF
MASTERMIND TALKS AND AUTHOR
OF *MASTERMIND DINNERS*

Mastermind Talks produces exclusive events geared toward entrepreneurs interested in peer support, health, and personal growth. I could have written an entire book about how

Gaignard has built a community around him. Luckily, he has written one already, Mastermind Dinners. He leverages events and dinners to build relationships and stay engaged and has curated an incredible sphere of influence of enviable household names, all while being an insanely humble and giving person.

Even the Most Experienced Professionals Still Think They May Fail

I've probably done well over a hundred dinners for sure. I still have that kind of feeling that this could be a huge failure. One thing that has been helpful, however, is to stack the cards in my favor. If I have an existing peer group, I'll invite those people first, and that will give me the vote of confidence I need before I start reaching out to people who I'm not as close with. If I'm trying to organize a dinner for 20 people, and I'm already close with the first 10 I invite, that makes it a lot easier for me.

As a young CEO, one of the most daunting tasks I had trouble with was reaching out and following up with potential investors. I was so worried about saying the wrong thing, of them saying no, of being rejected. One of my earliest mentors coached me on focusing my mind on just writing the best message possible. In fact, I assume that they are going to say no just to relax my mind. Don't worry about your action being a home run, a strike, or a line drive. Babe Ruth said, "Never let the fear of striking out keep you from playing the game." Just swing the bat as best as you can; that's all you can control.

When you've identified the appropriate action to take, it's time to switch off any thought or concern about the potential fallout, bad or good. Nuclear missiles, once launched, can't be recalled or diverted. You are doing this.

SOMETHING IS BETTER
THAN NOTHING

As we're thinking about adding value, we have to consider that any amount of value our recipient perceives is better than nothing.

I am using those words carefully. We want to ensure that value—any amount of value—is delivered. Being the eighty-fifth person to "like" a post will not stand out; in that case, your value is anonymized.

If the experience we create for our contact can be attributed to us by them, then anything is better than nothing.

If you were online in 2014, you may remember Yo. The app had one purpose. By pressing the name of one of your "friends" in the app, that person would receive a push notification saying, "Yo from _____." Yeah, that's it. And the developers raised a million dollars from some all-star investors. Bless capitalism. It was widely thought of as a toy, and while it was, it actually reduced to a subatomic level the concept of delivering value. When you received that notification on your phone, it showed that the sender was thinking about you. Even if just for a split second. People were thinking of you and thought it was worth expending a fraction of a calorie moving their finger to click on your name. That social connection was there. As social creatures, isn't that social connection one of our core drivers?

Now I'm not advocating that social networks should bring back the ability for you to "poke" all of your past clients. But as you are deciding the level of investment you are putting into engaging with a prioritized relationship, just keep in mind that the most minute impact may still move the needle—as long as it's personal (they know it's you), relevant, and authentic. Just a text message saying, "Hey, just thinking of you, hope all is well" is better than nothing. Sending a quick e-mail saying, "Hope things at Dunder Mifflin are great!" will show that you are expressing *some* level of concern for them.

MICHELLE LEDERMAN, AUTHOR OF *THE CONNECTOR'S ADVANTAGE*, *THE 11 LAWS OF LIKABILITY*, AND *NAIL THE INTERVIEW, LAND THE JOB*

One of the oft-forgotten ways of being likable is to just be honest and say you are reaching out to someone. Try not to come up with a reason. Simply say, "I was just thinking about you," and that will show people that they were on your mind and that you liked them enough to want to extend the connection.

If somebody keeps coming into my head, I simply tell the person, "You keep coming into my head, wondering what's going on with you." Or it may just be, "I ran into somebody, and they mentioned your name," or "I heard from so and so about _____ (fill in the blank) and wanted to hear more." It isn't coming up with a reason, it is sharing the actual reason.

I had done work for someone who was with a big finance company at the time. I heard through the grapevine that she had left and gotten a new job. The subject line of my e-mail to her was "Thinking about you." Keep in mind, both of us are professionals. It's no different than reaching out to a friend and saying, "Hey, thought of you." I kept the rest of the e-mail light. "You keep popping into my head. How's the new job going? Things are busy here. Would love to catch up when schedules allow." That was it.

I got three e-mails back.

When struggling with how we may come across, we should never hesitate to just be ourselves.

So long as we're not being annoying. There is of course an opposing boundary to keep in mind. While we should be comfortable with taking some level of action, when the action becomes so cheap or so frequent that it comes across as impersonal, inauthentic, or unvaluable, that's when we can risk *degrading* the relationship. The best counter to this is to reduce the frequency. That simple "checking in" e-mail is fine if it's sent once every 6 or 12 months.

The next time you're struggling with figuring out what to say, just keep in mind that even the most minute of actions can deliver the experience you're trying to get across. There are some sample templates for you to steal in Appendix C.

MEASURE YOUR INVESTMENT

We want to make sure that the level of effort we are expending is relative to the value we hope to receive. Here are a few ways to deliver value:

- Just saying hello, or letting your contacts know you're thinking of them
- Inquiring about any challenges they are encountering
- Sending a gift
- Meeting for a meal
- Sending a handwritten card
- Sending them information
- Providing something exclusive
- Making an introduction

All of these are good ideas, so which one do I pick?

The key concept to frame the answer to that is *balancing the amount of resources that item of value requires vs. the priority of that relationship.*

When we were talking about prioritizing our sphere into different tiers relative to their perceived value to us, it ties back to this.

Every one of those experience ideas will take different amounts of time, money, or other resources to accomplish.

- A quick "hello" text message takes seconds and has no variable cost (just your cell phone bill).

- Sending a handwritten note may just cost a few dollars in stationery and postage but may take 5 to 10 minutes of your time.

- Meeting for a meal can cost $50 to $100 plus two hours of your time (including travel).

- Making an e-mail introduction to another valued contact may take a few minutes and cost you nothing, other than the social capital that you've built up.

Now, let's say you actually paid attention when we were talking about prioritizing your network. Opening your database, you see 10 Top Clients, 20 Hot Prospects, 40 Past Clients, and 100 Web Leads.

Are you sending handwritten cards to all your web leads every six months while only texting your top clients once a quarter? In isolation, it's hard to determine whether each individual decision is a good or bad one, but *relative to each other*, one sees the stark difference, making the decision clear.

We want to *measure the total amount of effort we put into a relationship* to correlate to its priority in our sphere—and the number of similar people we have in that sphere.

There's no tried and true formula on "if I give, I get." *It depends on the person, the ask, and the situation.*

How would you order these?

- Sending a "thinking of you" message to a college friend

- Sending a logo-emblazoned mug to a wealthy business contact

- Buying lunch for a prospective customer

- Sending a past client a birthday card

You can't! There are too many variables and sociological uncertainties to deal with here. For example, rekindling a relationship with a college buddy could unlock a whole new network of amazing opportunities. The prospective customer gets taken out to lunch all the time. Or the past client's birthday is always forgotten, and he loves getting cards in the mail.

There is no hard and fast rule here, nor am I going to give you some arbitrary ratio ("you should spend five times as much time and money on your VIPs as you would on anyone else"). You are the master of your time, money, and other assets. It is completely up to you as to how to deploy it. But knowing that we each have varying—and finite—levels of resources, we should ensure we're doling them out effectively for maximum impact.

Here's an example of how you might distribute your efforts, given the prior example.

- 10 Top Clients—dinner out once every six months, followed by a handwritten card and personalized gift

- 20 Hot Prospects—handwritten card and a gift certificate to a neighborhood restaurant

- 40 Past Clients—annual gift and call every six months

- 100 Web Leads—the monthly newsletter and a quarterly phone call

One could spread the peanut butter evenly, but if you're betting on sports teams, would you place the same bet on every team winning, or put most of your money on the top 25?

CHRIS FRALIC, VENTURE CAPITALIST

For certain high-value, really unique, important connections, it's not crazy at all to put in that kind of investment in time to dig in and get to know your subject. Again, I think that doing any initial bit of research matters—e.g., if you're going to talk to a reporter, it would be good to have read through the last several articles that they have done to know how they think, what they're saying, what's published. That's a good level of research to do.

I was going to an event at Berkshire Hathaway in Omaha, Nebraska, and I saw that a senior executive I respect highly was going to be one of our hosts at a pre-conference event. I had been reading a book that shared a lot of his background, and learned a ton about him and his history, and was able to make some connections around him being the editor of *The Harvard Crimson*. After he spoke, I gave him a 1942 *Harvard Crimson* that I found as a thank you gift. He told me, "Wow. That's incredible." It was published during World War II, and he even noted, "Jack Kennedy was the editor in 1940."

It was a good way to make a good connection, and I did it from an authentic place. It shows that I care about understanding the person's background and came up with something thoughtful that stood out, and he appreciated it. I'm not asking for anything in particular from him right now, but I now have the connection and can follow up later at some point.

YOU WANT TO STAND OUT

If we're trying to stay engaged and remind contacts of our value to them and their value to us, we also have to keep in mind that we're not alone. We live in a world in which any advantages we had when it came to unique skills or knowledge have been eliminated, leaving our reputation as the best competitive advantage. We have to assume that we are not the only people vying for their attention—or business. How effective is a strong relationship when we don't stand out above the noise?

The good news is that there are some really well-worn paths when it comes to relationship building.

Every December, my lawyer—whom I love to death—sends me the same brick of chocolate. A giant bar with his firm's logo and a little hammer to break it. It's great; all the new employees get a thrill over it. But I've been receiving that identical gift for about 10 years. I know it's coming, as do our more tenured employees. It's expected. In fact, if I didn't receive it, I would be *offended*.

There's an industry conference I attend twice a year that has a stacked set of official and unofficial after parties. One of the bigger vendors has consistently hosted a huge bash. Every single time. It's now *expected*—the perceived value of the sponsorship is gone— so that when they decided to make it a more limited affair, people were *furious* at them.

We can, right here, right now, decide that we're going to zig when everyone comfortably zags. If we focus our efforts on separating ourselves from the pack, we can ensure that our message is received loud and clear. Per the prominent venture capitalist Peter Thiel, rather than striving to win in a crowded market, seek to differentiate yourself so you become a monopoly of one.

Spend your time understanding what your competition and everyone else is doing. Then, improve on it—or do something else.

That said, it doesn't mean you can't leverage what the best practice is and innovate on it.

You can choose a different opportunity to reach out. How many cards and other gifts do you get the last two weeks of the year? *Boring.* Skip the holiday card. As we mentioned, when it comes to timely engagement, choose a different holiday to celebrate, maybe in the dead of winter or the dog days of summer. There's a company in DC that doesn't do a holiday party for its employees but throws a huge Cinco de Mayo event for everyone and the community.

You can time shift. For example, when people change jobs, don't just send them a congratulatory e-mail. Everyone does that. Instead, send them an e-mail one month later, and again at one year into their new job, checking in on how they're liking the new opportunity.

Change channels. While I have a strong belief in e-mail being the universal platform for communicating between two professionals, that doesn't mean it is the *only* channel out there. Between e-mail, social media, postal mail, phone, in-person, there are so many methods to choose from. Changing things up can help you distinguish yourself.

One thing we weren't expecting when we started Contactually was how many people sent in product requests for *sending handwritten cards*. I thought they were out of their darned minds! When did my grandmother's bridge group sign up for an account? Then I received one from a customer, and it stood out that day.

Social media is great in that it has conditioned people to share any significant life event, in a semipublic forum. My wife and I didn't consider ourselves a couple until we became "Facebook-official" in college. Keep in mind that these social platforms rely on the positive feedback loop of likes and comments in order to incentivize us to craft the perfect post ASAP. As these social platforms are aiming for volume of posts and views on those posts, not the quality or attribution of who actually commented or liked, your digital vote of support may not get their attention.

So the next time you identify a post worthy of it, respond, just do it on a different channel. That text message, phone call, or even e-mail will register in a different way than yet another comment.[1]

Be a purple cow. Seth Godin, a master of marketing, wrote the seminal book *Purple Cow: Transform Your Business by Being Remarkable* about creative marketing—that you're either remarkable or you're invisible. How can you be remarkable? Better yet, how can your experience reflect your identity and how you want people to think of you? For example, instead of a wine tasting, how about a hot sauce tasting? Within reasonable bounds, how can you differentiate yourself as much as possible?

CHARLES BLACK, LUXURY REALTOR

The buyers that we work with are some of the most in-demand people around. When I think about what I can offer this segment of the market, time and knowledge are most important. There are certainly some basics: being responsive and following through on what you said you'll do. Trust can disappear in an instant. They look to me for my knowledge that others don't have—what's not yet on the market and the backstory for every property for sale. You may not think this is a big deal, but understanding *why* sellers are selling matters in this market.

We also have to go to where they are, which requires the right amount of intelligence about them, and keeping close track of it. We keep track of their preferred method of communication and leverage that, as well as the window of time that's best for them. Still, nothing is more important than face-to-face, which may be as simple as a meeting at the client's office, out for a cup of coffee, or courtside at a Lakers game. No matter what, we have to be the one working around their schedule, on their turf (their office, their preferred restaurant, their favorite sports venue), on their time. For all of these reasons, keeping very close tabs on every bit of intelligence in our CRM has been a critical practice.

YOUR GESTURE HAS TO BE MEANINGFUL, RELEVANT, AND VALUABLE

If we want to be perceived as valuable, then a strong pathway forward is to ensure that our engagement with our sphere of influence is meaningful in some way, and relevant to them and their current situation.

- **Meaningful.** Something that is important to the recipient that will be appreciated and remembered.

- **Relevant.** Relates to something that they (and ideally, you) care about.

- **Valuable.** Should add legitimate value to their life.

Now we see where the *I* in CAPITAL comes into play. We didn't just gather all of that intelligence for blackmail purposes. We can use this when we are reaching out. Even the slightest bit of personalization can register more powerfully.

Why? As social creatures, we seek that personal connection. We want to be *known*. We value people that we know. Better yet, we value people who know us. If we want to be perceived as valuable, we want to break into that personal world where they also feel valued by us.

When reaching out in a professional setting, a critical prerequisite is to recall any intelligence you have already accrued or can gather further, if your desired level of investment necessitates it. While intelligence is time-consuming to both gather and distill, leveraging that information can be automated (for example, can your database automatically drop in the company name and/or month you last spoke when sending an e-mail?), in which case that doesn't take any marginal effort. Taking what might otherwise be a boilerplate message and layering top key insights can help you remind people of the relationship you have (or desire to have), breaking through the defense mechanism of "is it worth responding to this message?" If you recall, for me, a cheap basketball was a home run relative to a rote "thanks for meeting, plz help me" e-mail.

JOHN CORCORAN, COFOUNDER OF RISE25

John Corcoran works with entrepreneurs of all types, helping them turn relationships into revenue. He is one of the best connectors I know.

I've seen so many people have confidence issues when trying to connect, particularly if it's with people who are at a higher stature than they are. Regardless of your place in the world, you can always connect at a human level. You can deliver tremendous value to someone and actually create a much stronger bond without talking about your core offering.

I was at a conference talking to someone who is one of the co-owners of a very large software company, a company with which we would like to create a partnership in the future. We didn't talk at all about anything related to business or work or behavior or anything like that. It turns out his son was in a home run hitting derby (his son's about the same age as my son). We started talking about little league teams, especially about travel teams. I started giving him recommendations on how to manage that situation, when your kids are traveling and you start getting busier and busier.

In that instance, it wasn't a long conversation, but I tried to steer it toward learning about the person as much as possible, and then see where I can deliver value outside of the work topic, outside of something related to my vocation. It's a better way of connecting with someone than if I were to try to force the conversation onto a business topic where I'm delivering some value around the work that I do.

Sometimes I'll take it a bit further and send a follow-up e-mail. Going that extra step makes the big difference with people. It's one thing to have that casual conversation, but it's another to follow up with someone and say, "I remember our conversation. I remember you said you're passionate about this particular topic, and I'm sending you a follow-up piece of information related to that thing."

Does your gift really need to have your logo? Are you trying to turn your contacts into walking billboards? What if the item had a story attached to it, whether personal to them or not?

I was in Chicago at an investor event. The speaker they had brought in was an excellent storyteller, and a master of relating his message through specific anecdotes. He told us the story of the Fisher Space Pen (I'll pause here to let you do a quick search), about the true origins of it versus the fable. As he was finishing the story, he asked all of us to reach under our chairs, where we found a Fisher Space Pen, which he noted was a gift to us. No company logo, no note. The *story about the gift* is what comes to mind every time I see the pen on my desk. Beats the hell out of a water bottle with your company logo on it. That pen now *means* something to me as I recall that experience.

TAKING ACTION

- How do I make sure that what I am sending or giving to contacts creates value between us? What is the feeling I want them to have about me?

- How much time, effort, and resources do I want to put into this relationship relative to its priority to me?

- What do I know about this person? What are the relevant details that could play a factor in making this meaningful and personal?

- What is the common and expected path to take here, and how do I deviate from that?

Then take action! Launch the missile!

When delivering value, there are a few methods we can employ depending on the *experiences* we want to create:

- The *Personal Experience* involves engaging one-on-one for a direct value transfer. This might be an e-mail, handwritten card, meeting, or gift.

- The *Connection Experience* means providing the link between two people and, by creating that new social connection, delivering value.

- The *Community Experience* builds on the connector experience. It magnifies the value others see in the connector and the social object around the connecting experience.

This could be as simple as hosting a dinner for a few interesting people.

- The *Broadcast Experience* involves publishing content, which, while delivering lower value, can be done for a wider audience. This is usually done using social media or e-mail lists.

Which one do I choose? *Our default should always be to build a personal, authentic relationship, so the Personal Experience is always the starting point.*

Beyond that, it's whatever you feel most comfortable with, with the right people.

For someone who doesn't drink coffee (I'm one of those immature fools who just never got used to the taste; I prefer a satchel of dried sticks and leaves dunked in hot water), I have a *lot* of coffee meetings. I spend time with people one-on-one and ask three core questions: What are you working on? What are your major challenges? How I can help?

Introductions are usually one of the main outputs of those meetings. I consider my advice to be one minor data point, so the best I can do to help them is expand my one-on-one relationship to one-on-one-on-many, where I'm connecting them to my network for further advice and help. If someone is working on a new public advocacy start-up, I'll connect them with a contact I have at a few consulting firms who focus on nonprofits. If someone's prototype is starting to see signs of life, I may connect that person

There are different ways to deliver value.

with my CFO or corporate counsel, both of whom I've worked with for years.

What I do consume in quantity is . . . hot sauce. I put hot sauce on everything. What I have been known to do periodically is bring over a bunch of loose connections, or strong connections I haven't seen in person in some time, to my office to taste different hot sauces. A tasty—and sometimes painful—experience.

A friend and I have also hosted an event called Battledecks (some know it as slideshow karaoke), at which attendees present in front of an audience a PowerPoint they've never seen before. The results are hilarious! Your improv skills are seriously tested when you're being asked to present a sales pitch for a tractor company, or medical best practices for cats with a UTI.

What do these four examples have to do with each other? They are all ways of delivering value. When I'm meeting with contacts one-on-one, I'm leveraging the direct mindset, giving them my full focus and attention. When I'm making introductions, the connection mindset delivers value by being the broker for another hopefully valuable relationship. With the latter two, I'm giving them a unique shared experience and delivering value by creating a community, even if I'm unable to engage with them one-on-one at that time. Hopefully, they'll walk out with some new relationships and social objects.

You may love hosting events and be the social butterfly in a roomful of people. Or you may prefer quieter, more intimate occasions. There is no right or wrong approach, as each has the potential to deliver the end result of improving how others perceive you. It depends on your style, the relationships you're looking to invest in and their personalities, how much time and effort you can dedicate, and your desired outcome.

QUICK WIN

Write down 10 specific ways you believe you can add value to your sphere.

KEY TAKEAWAYS

- Your goal in relationship marketing is not just to stay top of mind, it's to be valuable. Therefore, it's not about following up; it's about adding value.

- Every action you take with your sphere should be meaningful, relevant, and valuable.

- Seek to differentiate yourself, whether through shifting the date and time you engage, the channel you use, or the gift you give.

11

ADD VALUE, PART 2: OFFERING MORE THROUGH CONNECTION

THE PERSONAL, ONE-ON-ONE EXPERIENCE

Engaging with people one-on-one is where we spend most of our time, and where most value is exchanged. Our goal is to build a relationship where contacts perceive us as valuable, and put value on our relationship with them. There are a number of paths you can take to achieve the goal of increasing mindshare in a personalized way.

- People should feel that your outreach is *meaningful* to them.

- It should be *relevant* in some way.

- You want to come across as *authentic and personal*, otherwise you risk undermining the relationship.

- You have to actually press Send.

I'll bring up that last point throughout this book, as it's a key one. The biggest flaw I've seen is not poor tactics or sloppy execution; it's the absence of anything at all. I'll remind you of my earlier point to divorce the action from the result, and that something is better than nothing. Now we're going to step it up, from the very simple to the more complex.

Have you ever bought paint from a paint store? Spent hours arguing with your loved one about whether you wanted Sea Foam Blue or Ocean Glass, and the impact it was going to have on your child's development? Well, when you finally picked the right color out of the hundreds of options, you'll note that they don't have these premixed for you (can you imagine how many Indiana Jones–style warehouses they would need for that many variations?). Rather, the computerized paint mixer does this according to pre-set ratios to achieve the perfect shade of Cat Paw Brown to make your IKEA sofa pop.

When we're delivering personal value, we have a number of ingredients at our disposal.

- What channel or method do we want to use?

- How much do we want to leverage our intelligence on them?

- How much do we want to provide or demonstrate value?

- How much are we willing to spend?

With these components at our disposal, I'm going to lay out a number of general approaches that combine these.

Just Check In

There is nothing wrong with a simple ping to check in with someone. The only thing to keep in mind is *timing* and *response rate*. Under the guideline of making sure your communications are meaningful and authentic, sending the exact same e-mail every month, "Just checking in!" risks quickly showing the recipient that you don't really care about the response.

A good test is always to envision receiving the message yourself. *How would you respond?* The old adage of "try walking a mile in their shoes" applies here.[1]

One small tweak I've found to be helpful is to make it completely optional for them to actually respond to you. You're trying to evoke an emotional reaction most of the time, and that won't always necessitate a response. Frame your message in such a way that they don't need to respond to you. If appropriate, you can explicitly state "No need to respond" or NNTR. You're doing them a solid by relieving them of that burden.

You may deploy a wide variety of channels. Your default might be e-mail, but what about a message on a social network? Or text? Or a simple phone call? Whatever you choose has to be appropriate, without stepping over a line, like calling them on a weekend, or finding their profile on a dating site and sending them a personal message there (just to be clear, this is on the wrong side of the line). When selecting a channel, you can also use it to control which of their personas you are addressing. While an always-on society has blurred the line between who we are inside and outside of the office, our tone on a social gaming site will vary from what we use on our corporate e-mail. An e-mail to someone's work inbox is going to elicit a very different response than messaging them on their Pinterest profile.

These outreaches can be templatized and, if appropriate, automated. The foundational step is more about getting top of mind with them. Seeing that you are talking to them matters more than what message you are trying to deliver.

TONY CAPPAERT, COFOUNDER AND COO OF CONTACTUALLY

I try to build my life around processes and systems I can leverage to form ongoing habits. How I go about nurturing the people who matter most to me is no exception.

The biggest thing that initially held me back from regularly reaching out to my sphere was figuring out what to say. I knew who to talk to and when I needed to talk to them (it'd clearly been too long!), but Contactually handles that for me now. I struggled with what I could say that would be perceived as valuable.

Today, I use a few rules of thumb to help overcome this hurdle:

- Saying something—nearly anything!—is almost always better than saying nothing. If people know you and like you, they want to hear from you. Just saying something like "I was just thinking about you today . . ." goes a long way. If I know I need to follow up with someone, I'll default to a simple message to ensure they don't slip through the cracks.

- One of the best ways to rekindle an old relationship is to share a quick update on what you've been up to recently. I created a "Personal update" template that summarizes in a few bullet points the biggest personal and professional happenings in my life over the past three to six months. I use this as a starting place to create a more substantive check-in. Again, I follow the assumption these people know me, like me, and genuinely care what I've been up to. This provides an easy path for people to feel connected with me.

- When I first started regularly following up with my sphere, I found every follow-up I sent just created more work: more e-mails, phone calls, coffee dates, and lunches. And I felt uneasy that those same folks felt pressure to take action in return. Now, about half the time I wrap up with a quick "No need to reply to this e-mail; I know we're all busy! I just wanted to let you know I was thinking of you." It's like magic.

With these rules of thumb, I can quickly follow up with the people in my sphere, and do so in an authentic, intimate way. I block 30 minutes on my calendar every week and am quickly able to follow up with 10 to 12 people.

> For me, it's less about automation and more about using little hacks that enable me to follow through on my intention. Do these little things enough, and they become a habit.

When you're ready to kick it up a notch, that's when you . . .

Add Personalization

I must warn you that the forthcoming steps will increase the level of effort that you must make *per person*. If you recall our focus on prioritization, our higher priority relationships, which are fewer in number, should require the most time and resources.

Adding some personal details about the recipient hits multiple targets that amplify the feeling that we are *personally* interested and invested in them.

The most basic method of personalization is painfully obvious; address it to that person. Research has shown that people appreciate hearing their own name. You can step it up, of course. It's highly likely that you have their company name, too, or can easily find it.

When we're looking to personalize our outreach, this is when our intelligence comes in. If you need a refresher, I recommend you reread the chapter on Intelligence and review the tactics at the end.

At a high level, intelligence involves:

- Reviewing any notes and past conversations for key facts about them, their business, or their challenges.

- Leveraging any additional information your database has been able to pull about them.

- Searching online for any recent news or trends about them, their company, or the industry they work in.

- Analyzing what they've been posting about in social forums recently.

Go Where They Are

When building relationships one-on-one, it is not always about creating an interaction out of thin air. How can you interact with them where they already are?

Social networks are conducive to soliciting interactions. If they are active on a particular social network, that can be a perfect way to engage.

Don't just "like" though, engage! Post a comment that asks a question or encourages conversation. Show that you are genuinely interested in them and what they have going on in their life.

Or repost, rebroadcasting their content to your own social followers. Your contact is likely to see that you are lending your own credibility and social capital to what they have to say. As you're doing this, keep in mind the core intent. You're looking to maintain the relationship, show you care about them, and demonstrate value.

PETER LORIMER, FOUNDER OF PLG ESTATES

Peter Lorimer turned his successful career as a world-traveling music producer into a prolific boutique real estate agency, PLG Estates. His focus on high quality—whether in the properties he represents, the clientele he attracts, or the content he himself produces, is one of the many reasons why he's also the costar of the hit streaming show Stay Here.

There is a prevalent misconception that social media is something we get to when we've done everything else. That traditional tasks such as prospecting by phone and e-mail should take precedence over creating original, authentic content, which I feel couldn't be more inaccurate. As for me, the traditional methods of prospecting are evaporating in front of our eyes and being replaced by far more sophisticated strategies, such as Instagram, direct messages through Facebook, LinkedIn, and all the usual suspects. Far too often, I hear other people explain that social media is driving them crazy and they will get to it when they get to it, which in my opinion is just bashing a nail into the coffin of their career.

Face-to-Face Conversation: The Biggest Investment with the Biggest Impact

When it comes to keeping a vibrant relationship, in-person, face-to-face interactions, whether one-on-one at a coffee shop, at a networking event, or around a predictably oversized conference table are ideal.

SUSAN ROANE, AUTHOR OF
HOW TO WORK A ROOM

Susan RoAne is an in-demand speaker and podcast guest who shares her strategies for meeting, mixing, and mingling with business audiences worldwide.

The grease and glue of connections and relationships is conversation. While grease and glue have different properties and may seem to be polar opposites (one is slippery as in "greasing the wheel of words"; the other is sticky and binding), they are intertwined. The conversation of connection is an exchange of words, thoughts, suggestions, ideas, opinions, laughter (if we are lucky), and feelings that lay the groundwork—and build the foundation—of relationships.

If that exchange starts online via LinkedIn, Slack, Contactually, Twitter, or whatever the app du jour, moving it to a real-time exchange is valuable for connecting. Having written *How to Work a Room*, my belief has not wavered: meeting people in person is the ultimate. The value of face-to-face time cannot be underestimated. But, if geography makes that impossible, we now have access to a variety of tools that allow for global face-to-face even if it's not inperson. Whether we use Facetime, Skype, or WhatsApp, being able to see our conversational partners across the country or the globe is a bonus and a bridge to building long-term relationships.

EXCHANGING VALUE PHYSICALLY: THE GIFT

It's a normal Tuesday afternoon in our office, which means I'm bouncing around from meeting to meeting. At around 4 p.m., I finally have a short gap during which I can respond to some e-mails and catch up on internal chat messages. But when I get to my desk, I find a package. If your household resembles mine, then seeing a pile of boxes has become meaningless—likely just another shipment of dog food, dish detergent, or a mini-pallet of beans that were 30 cents off. But when it's at the office, addressed to you, the childhood magic of a present returns, especially when it's unexpected. Even getting a hand-addressed envelope can create a special moment.

If our goal is not just to stay top of mind but to demonstrate how a relationship with us is of value to someone in our sphere of influence, the inevitable tactic to consider is to throw down a credit card and buy something *of monetary value* for them.

Before you pop that $5.00 coffee gift card in the mail, ask yourself if it is meaningful, relevant, and valuable. It's easy to find ways to spend money on someone and think that we are giving them something of benefit to them. One could argue that one coffee you buy them is one coffee they don't have to buy themselves, meaning more money in their pocket. That certainly is valuable, but does that demonstrate that *we* are valuable? Is it *relevant* to them and our relationship? Will it *mean* something to them?

JOHN RUHLIN, AUTHOR OF *GIFTOLOGY*

It's hard for me to think about any kind of gifting without mentioning John Ruhlin, who has established himself as the go-to for strategic gifting. I highly recommend his book, Giftology.

We have to step back and think about the purpose of a gift first. As opposed to a marketing tool, a gift should be an artifact. The goal of an artifact is for something to create a mutual history. The gift should represent the value of the relationship. The gift should be not only an investment from a dollars perspective but an investment from a thoughtfulness perspective. The purpose of the gift is to make people feel as if they are important. As they use it in the following days, weeks, months, and years to come, it's a tangible trigger that reminds them of you, of that time, the emotion in that relationship. With all the noise these days, when you give what we call an artifact (not a gift), you're the most top-of-mind person in that person's world. More than anything, it's a reminder of the relationship and the power and the specialness of that relationship, so that's what we think of when we think of a gift in a business scenario.

Focus on the recipient. A gift by its very nature should be recipient-focused. We shop with our own eyes; we give for *their* own eyes. A gift is not an advertisement, meaning it should not have your logo or branding on it. When you try to turn it into an advertisement, you're actually making the gift icky. People read between the lines subconsciously and they're thinking, "Really, you're trying to disguise this marketing ploy as a gift?"

Failure is OK. If you are going to hand select a gift and spend hours, if not days or weeks, on every single gift, you're going to miss sometimes. People think I must be the perfect gift-giver. Talk to my wife. I suck sometimes. In all honesty, I'm trying to hit 8 or 9 out of 10.

And don't try for a perfect record, especially when you're gifting at scale. With a list of 100 people, what does everyone on that list have in common? Well, a lot of people have spouses, a lot of people like to eat food and drink wine, so we try to tie into things that are common among humanity. Most are surprised that knives have continued to be so popular. I know that if somebody is married, their spouses oftentimes are not included in any gift. Their assistant is usually treated like a pawn, not like a peer.

I try to take care of someone's inner circle 80 percent of the time if I can, because the bar is so low. Personalize the gift and maximize the number of people you reach. If you can make them say, "Wow, this is so thoughtful," you will have created a deeper connection with them.

Sending anything of value can be a sign, but we need to tread carefully, as we can risk *damaging* the relationship. Could something be so far from valuable that it subtracts value? Go back to that visualization of finding a package on your desk. Opening it, you find:

- An autographed vinyl record of The Beatles
- A $5.00 gift card for a major burger chain
- A bottle of wine from a vineyard local to the sender, encased in a wooden box
- A book, say, Simon Sinek's *Leaders Eat Last*
- A cheap plastic pen, with your logo on it

What is valuable? Especially when it comes to gifts of any monetary cost, the *perceived* value can be wildly off. All the more reason not just to think about the price tag to you, but the *experience* it will create. Think through these possible responses:

- If I'm a giant Paul McCartney fan, an autographed record will be encased in glass on my wall, where I can see it all the time. Even if I'm not a fan, at worst, I could sell it.

- Maybe there's a franchise of MajorBurgerChain nearby that I happen to frequent. But if I'm more of a white-tablecloth executive, is that really all that I'm worth to the sender?

- I *love* good wine, especially from regions I'm not familiar with. But I may be a recovering alcoholic or otherwise prohibited from drinking.

- Leaders are readers, so yes, this book is helpful. Even if I have already read it, it shows they know that I care about leadership.

- A cheap pen, seriously?

Having intelligence about our relationships ensures that the gift experience we are providing is truly something they will appreciate and cherish. If nothing else, by knowing the basic information about the person—company, industry, role, location—we can identify items that are generally applicable. This information includes their current life stage, the type of relationship we have with them, and insights from great relationship intelligence and meticulous notes.

While everything should be meaningful, relevant, and authentic to *the recipient*, gifts that show a personal touch are near universally applicable.

For instance, everyone reads—or should read. What are the hottest books for their industry? If summer is around the corner, pick your favorite beach read. If there's a book that you have found valuable, share that.

Old Bay is a particular seasoning mixture that some people in our region consume more than water, but it is rarely seen elsewhere. If, when building a relationship, I feel it's appropriate, I've been known to send a shaker of it in the mail to give contacts a taste of our region. If you are trying to share information about yourself, is there a local item that may shed a little bit more insight about *you*?

As with all aspects of adding value, the level of effort and resources that go into the gift should be measured relative to the value of the relationship. The key thing to keep in mind is that *their experience* of receiving a gift can deviate wildly. All the more reason to personalize.

And seriously, stop sending the pen with your logo. People have enough pens.

Offer Help and Solve Problems

One of the fundamental truths in relationship marketing is *getting what you want by helping others get what they want*. The act of *demonstrating the intent* that you want to help get what they want can, in isolation, be a valuable experience.

Is there anything you need help with?

This is the most basic question you can ask. However, it's a double-edged sword. Yes, I have no doubt that you are broaching that question with the genuine desire to help. That phrase, however, is overused, so can be seen as disingenuous. In addition, such a general question may make it burdensome for your associate to figure out how to answer. What are you offering to help with? Will you mow my lawn? Hire a new VP for me? Figure out what I'm having for dinner? Give me an additional $50,000 in investment capital?

The more specific you can be, the better. One of the skills you will hone as you deepen relationships is the ability to ask great questions. While I still believe that making that most basic inquiry is personal, meaningful, and authentic, try a better prompt:

- What is the biggest challenge you're facing in your business right now?

- What are we celebrating a year from now?[2]

- What is one mess in your life that you need solved?

- Who is one person you're looking to meet right now?

While it's common to openly solicit your coworkers for areas you can assist in (we use open-ended prompts for one-on-ones with direct reports, and a standard question when engineers hold their daily status meetings), rolling it out externally can make a world of difference. You are likely to get one of two responses:

- Wow, no, but I'll keep that in mind. Thanks!

- Actually, yes, what we're looking for is . . .

In either case, you've changed the game. It doesn't matter whether you're a lowly twentysomething talking to a seasoned vet, or an experienced professional talking to a new recruit. You are suddenly positioned as the one helping them.

You May Not Even Need to Ask

The best way to deliver value in a personal setting is to know what would help them without having to ask. This is where the relationship intelligence you have collected, or can collect on the fly, comes in.

BRAD LAMBERT, PRODUCER

How does one break into the competitive, cutthroat world of Hollywood producers, starting out as a freelance marketer in North Carolina?

I was a freshman in college, and I was friends with a running back for the Steelers, Willy. He had just won the Super Bowl in 2005. In 2007, he was the leading rusher in the NFL, and in the second to the last game he broke his leg, which cost him at least a six-figure bonus and all the accolades of winning the rushing title as an undrafted free agent.

He had everything he needed—money, family, house, a car. There was nothing he needed that I could provide him. As an injured athlete, though, he was crushed. As an athlete, when you can't do what you were put on this earth to do—run the football and score touchdowns on Sundays—you lose your purpose. He fell into a dark place, and he had to get on that road to recovery.

I was just a crazy freshman in college, and I was like, "What can I do? What can I offer him that he can't do himself? . . . I'm going to set him up with his idol, Michael Jordan." I knew Willy. I knew what he cared about, what was lacking, where the opportunity was. He had never met Michael Jordan. I didn't tell him. I just started making calls, networking, trying to get in touch with the right people.

About two months after breaking his leg, he and his entire family went to a show at an LA Lakers game in Charlotte, an experience I was able to arrange. He went up there and spent the game with Michael Jordan. It was one of the coolest moments ever. These people have pretty much everything they could want, but how you get in the door is you don't treat them like that. You don't go in with your hand out, asking for stuff. You just treat them like a normal person; you offer value. You don't become a fanboy and act crazy.

Here are key questions I recommend you ask yourself as you're rifling through information to find the best possible way to help people:

- What was your contact's goal for the year the last time you spoke to them?

- What is most valuable to people in their industry?

- Looking at job boards or their website, is their company hiring right now?

- Have they just gone through a life event, such as a marriage, new child, new town?

- Have they just changed roles or companies?

- What are the normal challenges facing someone in that role (e.g., a Realtor is always looking for better marketing tactics, and a CEO is always looking for leadership insights)?

- Has there been any negative news posted about their company or industry recently?

- Are they working on any projects at the moment?

JAYSON GAIGNARD, FOUNDER OF MASTERMIND TALKS AND AUTHOR OF *MASTERMIND DINNERS*

One of my core principles when it comes to investing in relationships is the Biggest Fan Philosophy (I may come up with a better name in the future). Marketers have an innate ability to be in the shoes of a prospect and understand their wants, needs, and desires, often better than the consumer does. I've taken that approach to relationship building. I try to get a better understanding of what people's fears are, specifically, and try to be their biggest fan or their biggest supporter in those times when they're vulnerable.

When a friend launches a book, I put myself in their shoes and realize they are most likely thinking, "What happens if nobody buys any copies? What happens if nobody leaves reviews? What happens if people leave reviews, but they're negative reviews?" I ask myself, how can I be that person's biggest fan in that time period. I'll buy a bulk order of books, post on social media, and e-mail my list. When the book comes out, I'm often the first person who leaves a review on Amazon.

I don't care how successful you are as an author. You're checking that Amazon page a couple of times a day at least in that first week, and that matters. Those are ways to invest. When people are most vulnerable, being their biggest fan or their first supporter goes a really, really long way as far as investing in them. That's the Biggest Fan Philosophy.

I was in California at a summit of other industry executives. It was clearly established that a transactional attitude was unwelcome, so it was all about relationships. There, I met Linda, who turned out to lead a company that we had long desired to work with. We had a deep conversation about what our respective goals were for the year. She mentioned, among other things, that she was really excited about wanting to work on a book but had no idea where to begin other than jotting down scattered thoughts. Not having a clear next step from the conversation, we parted ways with each other's contact information, and I wrote down my notes. She, knowing me primarily as a leader of a software company, would have no idea that I was at the time writing this book and knew of an excellent editor (no, my editor did not make me say this). Unprompted, I reached out to her and asked if she would like an introduction to an editor I trusted. She exuberantly took me up on my offer and has continued to be thankful for that act.

Or Ask for a Favor Yourself

Yes, you read right. If you want to increase rapport, one potential solution is to ask *them* to do a favor for *you*. What?

> *He that has once done you a kindness will be more ready to do you another than he whom you yourself have obliged.*
> **—BENJAMIN FRANKLIN**

Oh, Ben, you naughty contrarian! The aptly named "Ben Franklin Effect" is a psychological occurrence in which someone who has done you a favor is more likely to do another one than is someone who has received a favor from you. Researchers have identified two potential reasons:

- Performing a favor for you increases their subconscious impression of you. They wouldn't do it if they hated you, right? So if they do the action, they must think highly of you.

- Alternatively, the one doing the asking is demonstrating their favoritism toward the one being asked, and vice versa.

JON LEVY, HUMAN BEHAVIORAL SCIENTIST AND AUTHOR OF *THE 2 A.M. PRINCIPLE*

Jon Levy is not only known for his globe-trotting adventures; he is viewed by many as one of the better curators of people (via his well-known international dinners and salons).

In the early days of my career, I would take immense pride in the fact that I didn't ask people for favors. I had this misconception that I was only really successful if no one helped me. Part of it was the arrogance that comes with youth, but regardless of the reason, I didn't realize that by trying to do everything solo, I was doing an incredible disservice to myself and my friends.

That mindset changed when I read Benjamin Franklin's autobiography. Rather than trying to win a political adversary over by being nice, Franklin asked the gentleman for a favor: to borrow a rare book from his library. After the gentleman invested effort in Franklin by delivering this rare book, the two ended up becoming lifelong friends.

The Ikea Effect

Scientific research has overwhelmingly shown that when you do someone else a favor, you tend to like that person more. In one study, a team of researchers led by Michael Norton, Daniel Mochon, and Dan Ariely found that people valued their IKEA furniture more than its actual worth because they had put time and effort into building it. It's known as the IKEA effect,[3] and it's similar when building relationships. The more you invest in someone, the more you care about them.

This doesn't mean you should walk up to people asking to borrow a million dollars. The key to asking for favors is to prioritize them from small to large. If you ask people for directions, ask them for the time first. It significantly improves the chances that they will give directions.

Once people put an initial investment into you by doing you a favor, they view you as a person worth the effort. Asking for favors was key to how I built The Influencers, a private community of over 1,500 thought leaders and tastemakers, ranging from award-winning musicians and actors to Nobel laureates and Olympic athletes. I accomplished this by inviting people 12 at a time to cook dinner together. The effort of preparing a meal with a group of strangers allows for the Ikea/Ben Franklin effect to kick in, and for everyone to bond more quickly. The fact is that any joint activity would work, from volunteering to painting, hiking, or team sports.

In the early days I started by inviting friends, and after the dinner I would ask for recommendations. As the dinners continued and word of mouth spread, the attendance list became more prestigious.

For those of you out there who feel like you need to do it all yourself, you don't. This belief could actually be holding you back. Instead, go out there, ask for help. Chances are you will end up with deeper and more meaningful relationships, and much further along in your career.

CREATING VALUE BY MAKING CONNECTIONS

How can we create a *win-win-win* situation? By introducing two people you know to each other, you get 1 + 1 = 3. Each of the recipients is receiving value as they now have a new connection who can open new doors for them. And you get bonus points for being the one to make the introduction.

Keep in mind that when making the introduction, the perceived value can be very different for each side.

- Connecting a homeowner to a plumber is valuable to both; each wants the connection.

- But if a vendor asks to be introduced to someone you're connected to on LinkedIn, the recipient may not be looking for their services. In fact, the introduction may be unwelcome.

You might want to do some initial vetting yourself. And that's why the best practice is to use the *double opt-in* introduction method, in which you ask permission of each party before making the introduction.

In other scenarios, inviting two people who could potentially help each other to meet with you in person can create a more intimate experience and better establish you as the broker of such a relationship.

CREATING VALUE BY BRINGING OTHERS TOGETHER WITH A COMMUNITY EXPERIENCE

Most of our engagement happens one-on-one. However, there are some really strong arguments for creating a group experience that I hope you consider.

First—and most obvious—you're able to build up mindshare with a lot of relationships at once. A one-hour meal with one person could instead be a two-hour dinner with 10 people. You'll likely engage with each attendee for only a few minutes, if at all, rather than having to come up with an entire hour's worth of conversation. When we host dinners for customers, I may only talk to people on their way in and out, but clearly they are engaged in conversation with others the rest of the night.

The *experience* itself is the gift. It almost doesn't matter if you were there yourself and spent time with them. It's about the value they receive from us. The social object is formed out of the conversations had, new connections made, and memories generated.

SHAY HATA, REALTOR

We always look for ways that we can scale up our ability to stay close with our clients in ways that may or may not seem unique, but have been effective in helping us build relationships. We'll rent out indoor play places to let kids unleash energy during miserable Chicago winters, invite all the ladies to a blowout salon, rent out movie theaters for new showings. All things we do to genuinely build relationships with the people we care about, many of whom will be working with us in the future.

The types of group experiences you create can fall into some common buckets: a breakfast, lunch, dinner, or cocktail event. But before you go and book a room at a hotel bar, keep in mind a few things:

Create a Real Experience

Just as with an e-mail or a coffee meeting, we are trying to deliver a valuable experience to them. How you create and execute the experience in every way can make an impact that, for better or worse, will make it onto the permanent record of your relationship. If you're not a detail-oriented person, this is the time to stretch your muscles, or seek help from a team member or professional event planner to help facilitate the event.

In my years of creating events, I've made many mistakes. As an attendee, I've been to some terrible events, too.

- How valuable is it to go to a five-star restaurant with a celebrity chef when your tablemates turn out to be the most depressing people imaginable, and you're getting pitched by some sponsor who has zero relevance to you?

- What about being invited to a networking event with other executives at a swanky bar, but lacking a private space for the event, so you don't know if you're talking to a CEO, an attendee of another conference entirely, or a traveling consultant?

- Or how about bringing an entire group of people to a gorgeous mansion in Virginia for a couple of days, and hiring a champion Frisbee instructor to teach you tricks outside, only to be stuck inside on a rainy afternoon? Actually, this is a personal example of *such* a terrible experience that we now joke about it. It's become a social object.

DEREK COBURN, WEALTH MANAGER AND COFOUNDER OF CADRE

We never use hotel ballrooms. That's the traditional default for a lot of people. We find really great theaters, really cool, unique, interesting spaces that just feel different. We've hosted events at the DC Improv, at piano bars, at theaters. That adds a certain element that has people feel more like they're participating in an experience and less like they're attending a traditional event.

Just please, please, please don't create yet another "networking event."

Who Is There Can Make or Break an Event

I think we've all been there, where we sit down next to someone, and for the next hour, we're fighting off periods of awkward silence with random bits of painfully extracted small talk. Most of us could do with better conversational skills (some prepared questions?). Let's not forget, however, that this could have been prevented had the organizer done a better job of curating the guest list.

The total number of people you invite can affect how loud or cramped the room is. Do you want everyone to be sitting together and having one conversation, or are people going to be divided up into different tables? Do you want a prominent executive sitting next to someone looking for a job? And let's face it, some people are just *not* good guests, and you're best just one-on-one with them.

JAYSON GAIGNARD, FOUNDER OF MASTERMIND TALKS AND AUTHOR OF *MASTERMIND DINNERS*

All the heavy lifting happens at the beginning, and it really comes down to the curation of the people. A dinner is like making a whole bunch of introductions. You want to ensure that every introduction you make is relevant.

The one thing I focus on is our uncommon commonalities, the similarities between two people that may not be visible if you just know their name and industry. The deeper the uncommon commonalities that two people share, the deeper the bond. If I can, I actually get people to fill out biographical forms before the dinner, which helps a lot with this process.

Having then gained intelligence on everyone, assigned seating is key. For example, for the dinner I did in LA, I sat two guys across from each other who are both entrepreneurs, but they're both also former professional mountain bikers. They didn't know it, but when they sit across from each other, there's a lot that they can talk about. They can talk about business, they can talk about mountain biking, they can talk about family. Even though all those I may gather together are entrepreneurs and influencers from different industries, they can swap notes and best practices.

If you're at a dinner and you're surrounded by people who are accountants, financial planners, and entrepreneurs, you may get along, you may hit it off, and you may be lucky enough to sit next to somebody with whom you share some commonalities outside of what you do professionally and have a great conversation. Unless you, the curator of the event, are intentional, you are creating risk that two people sitting next to each other won't enjoy it.

Seek to Be Different

For some, it's a common business development tactic to book a private room, invite a bunch of people they want to curry favor with, and throw in some steaks or mini hot dogs and copious amounts of alcohol.

There is a time and place for that, for sure. But I hate to say, for most people, saving them a few bucks on having to pay for dinner that night is not really seen as valuable. How can you create a unique experience that stands out, or becomes so unforgettable that they'll always think of you?

Shake up the Guest List to Spark Lively Discussion and Create Unexpected Connections

A corporate lawyer's clients and prospects are going to be corporate executives, so that's likely who will be on your RSVP list. If you're a mortgage broker, you're inviting real estate brokers to dinner. The professional events I host are normally with CEOs, investors, customers, or industry influencers. Very rarely are the groups intermixed. Thankfully the, worlds each group operates in are exciting enough that there is plenty to talk about beyond name, rank, and serial number. But if you want to consider stepping it up, and having the conversation be about something other than business transactions and common topics for your industry, then introducing some variety into your guest list can really throw your night off balance—in a good way.

Jon Levy's salons are valuable almost *exclusively* because of the wide variety of people Jon brings in.

Let the Venue Set Your Event Apart

If we're trying to create an experience, the environment that we're in can make the difference. Don't go the safe route of picking a milquetoast bar that could be in any city, or a restaurant that serves bland food to not upset anyone's stomachs or taste buds.

Be different.

If you are thinking about hosting a dinner, instead of jumping on a restaurant directory and filtering for private rooms and a good number of reviews, what about going on Airbnb and finding a gorgeous loft apartment that you can rent for one night? Bring in a private chef who talks to the guests about the food she's making while everyone watches, and one or two waitstaff to help out? Or maybe, hand everyone an apron as they walk in, and ask them to pitch in?

We're trying to create an attractive experience that allows people to better connect.

Choose an Activity That They Would Never Think of Doing or Never Be Able to Do

Yes, you could do a dinner. Or invite people for lunch and have some table topics. Or put a few hundred dollars on a bar tab. Maybe a wine tasting! But if those options strike you as *boooring*, deviate from the usual. This is where you have creative license to really tap into who you are and what you like to do and see if some or all of your tribe is willing to play ball. I am thankful (maybe?) to be invited to a ton of dinners and networking events of a few different varieties, and I attend a small subset of them. However, there were a number of people I've wanted to reconnect with and sought to create an event for them. Dinner? Nah. Wine? Don't drink it. Whiskey? Cohosted one the other week.

But I *do* love hot sauce.

Spending most of the night cradling my newborn daughter in my arms gave me a ton of time to watch videos online—and wow, did YouTube's recommendation engine take me down some weird rabbit holes. Among the many clips of *The Wire*, every performance of the Jabbawockeez (watch them, they're mesmerizing), or mini-documentaries about ship breaking, I watched one show where celebrities were brought on to try a sequence of consecutively hotter hot sauces and answer interview questions while their mouth was on fire.

So I bought all the hot sauces, wrote up some fun questions, and invited a group of people over, most of whom didn't know each other.

Everyone walked out thick as thieves. Why?

Because, through the pain, sweating, and in-the-moment hatred toward me for convincing them to do this, they all had a *shared experience*. Our friends are our friends, in part, because we've been through enough with them to have built up a library of memories. That evening, we all know how each one acted and reacted. We saw through the facade that we would put up in any other context. That mini-community existed, if only for one night, and remnants of it would remain forever. And you're the person who introduced that and gave them a new life experience.

Also, did you know that capsaicin (the chemical in peppers responsible for the heat) also causes our body to release enough dopamine to give you a runner's high? I'm sure that helped bonding, too, in a completely legal way.

Admittedly, the cost may go up (although you'd be surprised sometimes) with some of these ideas. And the amount of work and risk of failure increases.

You could, of course, introduce some variety to the standard formula, while still remaining conservative. We were hosting a dinner for our customers in New York, and while we evaluated yet another pretentious French brasserie or standard upscale Italian spot, we ended up bringing everyone to a Brazilian steakhouse, which everyone loved.

Having a program for a dinner or lunch can also make it special. For years, our friends have had the tradition at dinner parties of having everyone go around and share the highs and lows of their week, and what they're excited about next week. You can open up the conversation at a table by having everyone share one fact no one else at the table knows about them, their favorite elementary school teacher, or one thing they learned this week.

CHRIS SCHEMBRA, FOUNDER AND "CHIEF QUESTION ASKER" OF 7:47

Chris Schembra was able to take his background in theater, his desire to build deep relationships, and a great new pasta sauce recipe and create a phenomenon in New York City.

Taking the Dinner Deeper

Breaking bread together is already a strong way to establish common bonds. But if you're looking to get more advanced, creating space for people to open up and connect on a deeper level can ensure that your event—and you—are unforgettable.

What we're really talking about centers on shared activities and shared passions. Our dinners haven't changed from the inception, when I invited 20 people over to my home to feed them my new pasta sauce recipe to see if it was good or not. I had them arrive at 6:30 p.m. *sharp*. Because I was a lazy fella, I delegated tasks and empowered the attendees to work together to create the meal. Those shared activities, those bonding experiences over a task that we would all share, ended up creating a deep connection, which we've now replicated hundreds of times.

We start with cocktail hour. Then delegated tasks start at 7:47. We sit down to dinner at 8:00. We have dessert at 8:30. We open up communal discussion on particular topics at 8:35. Because we've spent two hours and five minutes preparing the community for that connection, they are ready to share.

Brené Brown does a wonderful job of explaining that vulnerability used to be seen as a weakness in a social setting, but now it's used as a connection tool. During this communal discussion, we would keep the topics focused away from work. Whether it's employees of the same company, clients, total strangers, or lifelong friends, what we often don't talk about are the deeply vulnerable topics. Everybody talks about surface-level stuff. We hate surface-level stuff. It's actually that deep human element that will set people's relationships apart. It falls on the dinner moderator to facilitate deep communal discussion.

I don't expect everyone to be able to take on that task, as it requires a deep level of empathy, and willingness to push people well out of the comfort zone of superficial talk. Just to be clear, we don't initially ask people to express their own vulnerabilities; we get them talking about other people through gratitude, and that creates that openness. One of the favorite questions we ask is, "If you could give credit or thanks to one person in your life that you don't give enough credit or thanks to, who would that be?" Anyone can answer that.

Yes, of course there are more professional table topics that you can pursue. Those work, too. Having everyone share one service they can provide for everyone, one ask they are looking for, one professional challenge—those can help facilitate exchanges of value among your attendees, which of course helps you, too. Our intent is to build personal and authentic relationships, and helping people open up and connect to each other on a deeper level helps that.

JOHN CORCORAN, COFOUNDER OF RISE25

There's a distinction between you being the knowledgeable guru and you connecting people with others who they want to connect with in their field. I don't proclaim to be the know-all-be-all guru who stands at the front of the room and has the answer to all questions. The key thing to remember: A players want to be with A players. The star students want to be in a room with other star students. More often they are not, or they have trouble finding those opportunities to be with other star students, who are at their level or slightly above.

Sometimes, people forget that they don't need to have all the answers, or the expertise. They forget that they can serve as a connector, even if it's in a smaller way. They get stuck thinking, "I'm a photographer," or "I'm a web designer" or "I'm a marketer," or "I'm a chiropractor," or "I'm a lawyer." Therefore, the only value I can deliver is related to what I do. You can deliver value related to connecting them with other people whom they want to know. It's especially helpful when you're early in your career and you don't have much authority. You don't have to have decades of experience and expertise under your belt because connecting people is an alternative way of delivering value.

REACHING A WIDER AUDIENCE
WITH A BROADCAST EXPERIENCE

I've noticed a pattern emerge as Contactually has grown. Our user base of, among other populations, residential real estate agents, has grown exponentially over the years. So has the number of biannual e-mails reminding me to adjust my clock for daylight savings. Now, maybe they know something about *me* that I don't, but *I always remember to adjust my clocks*. My devices do it all for me. The many senders here aren't sitting around thinking, *Oh, Zvi would definitely benefit from a reminder*. Instead, I'm just one of many people that they think may reciprocate some kind of value in exchange for a tiny bit of effort from them.

The *broadcast mindset* is all about delivering value to a larger audience, with little if any tailoring. I get a ton of holiday cards, advice on how to winterize my home, recipes for Grandma's famous chili, and restaurant recommendations. I log on to social media, and my feed is chock-full of content that people I know thought would be helpful to anyone they knew.

Those of you who have a marketing hat that you put on occasionally may think that a lot of this sounds like content marketing. Content marketing, according to the aptly named *Content Marketing Institute*, is "a strategic marketing approach focused on creating and distributing valuable, relevant, and consistent content to attract and retain a clearly defined audience—and, ultimately, to drive profitable customer action."

Sounds applicable to what we're doing, and it doesn't necessarily require, as its name may invoke to many, a dedicated set of writers churning out whitepapers and technical documents. It's delivering valuable content to a defined group of people.

So when I'm receiving that flurry of "don't forget to set your clock back/forward tonight!" messages, it's because someone added me to a list of similar people (usually prospective buyers, sellers, or referral sources) they want to build a relationship with. Delivering some kind of value, however minor, will help increase mindshare with this group. An obvious thing that an agent can talk about is the need to change your clocks twice a year, about the only time we realize that our microwave and car dashboards have a clock in them. I may be overly critical here—it is an attempt to deliver some kind of value, even though I know it's not necessarily targeted to me.

This is where the groupings of relationships that we've prioritized come into play. When thinking of that part of your sphere, ask:

- Would they be even somewhat receptive to something they know wasn't from me directly?

- What kind of value could I deliver to all of them in one fell swoop?

- What would show my resourcefulness or knowledge and leave a good impression?

- What could I do to give my sphere a view into my own life so they feel more connected to me when I engage personally?

Often, the higher-tiered the relationship, the greater the likelihood that impersonal communication may backfire.

For a very short period of time, I engaged in what I thought was a relatively harmless practice of taking my database and e-mailing all my contacts updates and some resources I had found helpful for one reason or another. While in general I received good responses to this, I also was rebuked by people I really did care about for sending something so impersonal, so I stopped. Instead, I've redoubled my efforts, for those relationships, on personal engagement.

If you decide that broadcasting value to a group of people is the right tactic to take, ask yourself:

What valuable, and relevant-to-our-relationship material can I deliver to this larger audience?

It has to be valuable. While some may honestly appreciate the deal or discount you're offering on your services, it should be something that, in pure isolation, will be valued by your target audience.

It should be relevant to the type of relationship you have with them based on their industry and the past, current, or, most important, desired association they have to you. You want to channel your expertise and usefulness, if nothing else, as a teaser for what further utility you can provide, should a deeper relationship blossom.

- A real estate agent shares her recommendations of up-and-coming restaurants in a neighborhood. It's always helpful to gain "the inside track," so it's valuable. And if this agent knows so much about this new neighborhood, maybe she knows about some properties that might be right for me.

- A lawyer shares his explanation and perspective of a court ruling relevant to the type of law he practices for clients.

- A consultant puts together some timely insights of trends she has noticed in the market she and her clients are in.

PETER CORBETT, FOUNDER OF ISTRATEGYLABS

Peter Corbett founded iStrategyLabs, an award winning-digital agency, in his apartment, and it was eventually acquired by WPP, one of the largest global advertising firms. There's a pretty well-worn playbook he could have followed: hire some designers and developers and do whatever clients asked him to do. Peter and his team never accepted that.

I've always been an e-mail hacker, using e-mail in special little ways to gain an edge. You can achieve a lot if you've got a lot of e-mail addresses of people who are interested in what you're up to.

When I was an undergrad at Emory University, a buddy and I decided it would be fun and very lucrative to go into the concert and club promotion business. How could we let all the Emory students know which club to go to so we could collect their cover charge at the door? Well, I figured out how to access the all-school e-mail listserv at Emory and proceeded to e-mail something like 40,000 people about a club promotion that coming Thursday. In short, we packed the club and made a ton of money, but the systems administrators of the school were really pissed (this would definitely be considered spam these days!).

Now, it's better to use e-mail in a more "on the up and up" kind of way if you're going to build a real business for the long term. Fast-forward 10 years later, and I'm the CEO of a growing digital agency called iStrategyLabs. I'm the proud owner of my very own e-mail list of about 30,000 which I've collected over the years through networking/ smart marketing online. One fine May, I was starting to get a bit concerned that our sales pipeline seemed a little light. Looking at my database, I asked myself, "Is there anyone in that 30,000-person list who might need our help?"

Now, I certainly wanted potential clients to reach out, but I also didn't care if it was financially beneficial. I just thought it would be fun to ask 30,000 people what help they needed, and see what happens. So I did. I e-mailed the list with the subject line "How can I help?" and one line of body copy that said "Let me know what you're up to and how I can help. Your friend, Peter" or something like that. Thousands and thousands of people responded, and I helped them all.

- "I'm looking for a node.js developer. Do you know one?" A five-minute favor, for sure.
- "I'm trying to start a luxury hand soap business. Can I come by and get a sense of how you'd market it?" Potential future customer.
- "Do you know anyone who's willing to build a website and marketing campaign for $250,000 in three months' time?" Immediate opportunity!

We closed about 10 percent of the year's revenue in the next month from people who reached out with a project. They did in fact want to pay us to help them! As an added bonus, the local business newspaper wrote about our approach!

There are some ways to bridge the "mass" with the "personalized." I recall working for a couple of nonprofits in college that would send out the standard form letter, thanking someone for their donation. But if the envelope stuffer or director would come across a familiar name, they'd scrawl a personal note.

That's what we ended up building out with Scalemail (there are a few other products that can do the same). Seeing a gap between sending a single message or having to CC/BCC a group of people, we invested time in a solution that was a hybrid of both. You would write one message to be sent to a group of people and, right before the final send, the system would personalize it appropriately, and let you do the same. So while the bulk of the message may be the same, you'd have the ability to drop in a personal tweak to the appropriate ones. The recipients will receive a message directly addressed to them, without any idea that others received a very similar message.

That's one-on-one relationships at scale, which will make it easier to achieve our relationship marketing goals.

A Broadcast Can Lead to Deeper Engagement

Your broadcast efforts don't have to be the beginning and end of the value delivery to that audience, far from it. Even with prioritization, you may still end up with too large an audience to personally deliver the desired level of value. One method to help narrow it down is to leverage a value broadcast, determine who is engaging, and then target that subset with a deeper message.

Who is liking my posts? The creators of most of our social media watering holes have trained us to engage with any content we approve or disprove of to a certain extent, and they make it as frictionless as possible to engage. It's hard to believe there was a time when you would simply consume content without the pressure to like or repost it. I'm always surprised by the nonobvious people I notice engaging with my content regularly. Clearly, what I'm sharing is resonating with them, or they are, consciously or not, demonstrating their favor toward me. That gives me the signal that they are people who would likely "pick up the phone" if I reached out.

Who is engaging with my messages? Whatever platform or CRM you are using to send messages, there is usually some way to send out your message with the ability to, unbeknownst to anyone other than an expert, track how your recipients interact with that message. That system might embed a near-invisible image that, by being downloaded by your e-mail client, signals that the person opened the message. Or by changing the links you embed in the message, will send the user to a third-party website for a split second before redirecting their browser to the intended site—just long enough for that intermediate server to identify which link in which e-mail was clicked on. Finally, by tracking incoming messages to your e-mail account, whether manually or technologically, you can see who is responding.

BE WORTH KNOWING

Throughout this book, we've talked about the need to be personal in your outreach. Being authentic in your communications. Being relevant to people in some way. One underlying prerequisite is to ensure that you are, in fact, relevant to them. It's of little use if we spend all of this time working to engage them, build value, and be successful if it turns out that we have done little work to actually differentiate ourselves from the other professionals who may be doing the same.

It's critical to differentiate ourselves in a commoditized market and stand out as *chocolate in a world of vanilla.*

DORIE CLARK, ADJUNCT PROFESSOR AT DUKE UNIVERSITY FUQUA SCHOOL OF BUSINESS, AND AUTHOR OF *ENTREPRENEURIAL YOU* AND *STAND OUT*

How can you stand out as someone interesting, and not "yet another businessperson"? One of the oft-ignored, yet incredibly valuable aspects to keep in mind is to be worth knowing.

The first and best way is to work on developing your visibility to the point that they've already heard of you by the time you engage personally. It's always easier for someone to get excited about meeting you if your name is familiar. That could be because you've created content for publications they read, have taken on a leadership role in an organization they're involved with, or perhaps you've had mutual friends talk you up and say you have a lot in common and really need to connect.

Beyond establishing a larger presence, cultivate elements of your personality or experiences that are unusual or would be especially interesting to that person. When people are asked, "So what have you been up to lately?" at events, most often they waste the opportunity and say, "Nothing much" or "Keeping busy." Instead, make sure you have something interesting to contribute, such as talking about learning a new skill or a travel destination you've recently visited. That sets you apart as someone who is seeking out new knowledge, and it makes you compelling for high-level people to know.

Ensuring you stand out can, and should, start well before the personal engagement. What makes you and your service offering unique and special? How do you communicate that to the outside world?

GETTING TACTICAL

- Choose whether you are seeking to add value by engaging directly, by creating a communal gathering, or by broadcasting.

- If adding value directly, do not be afraid to, if nothing else, check in and simply share that you're thinking of them.

- Leverage the intelligence you've gained on your contacts to identify areas you can help them or to recall some personal details to demonstrate your personal investment.

- Add value by solving personal or professional challenges, potentially through introductions.

- Do not hesitate to glean insights directly from them on how you can help by leveraging the right questions—or seek help from them.

- Gifts and physical items are powerful. However, make sure these are meaningful, relevant, and valuable to them.

- Add value by hosting and inviting people to an event. This can be as simple as a lunch or dinner. However, take time and care to curate the attendee list, select the right venue, and create the right environment for people to build deep relationships, not just exchange contact information.

QUICK WIN

Text five past clients or colleagues that you are "Just thinking of you. Hope all is well."

KEY TAKEAWAYS

- Adding value can be done individually by connecting people with others, by creating a community environment, or by broadcasting information to a larger audience.

- Your goal is to be personal, meaningful, and relevant to them. That is accomplished the moment you add value.

LEVERAGE: EXECUTING MORE EFFICIENTLY

It was early 2011 when I decided I needed to be more intentional about tracking my business development and relationships in general, a journey that would lead to the founding of Contactually later that year. I knew that I would be best served by, *at least*, writing down the opportunities I was working on and the relevant people associated with these opportunities. But as I tried for months and iterated through different software, I kept failing.

Was it because it was impossible? No. Hard? Not really. It was just a lot of work. I failed because I did other things with the time that could have been allotted toward my nascent relationship marketing practices. The core idea was birthed around the fact that I was "lazy" and wanted software to handle a bunch of the stuff I just wasn't motivated to do. Call it "lazy" or "efficient," a consistent theme professionally is the drive to do more in less time (so we can do even more, or just so we can rewatch *The West Wing* for the eighteenth time).

Most of what we've talked about in this book isn't cognitively challenging to do. Actually, I would say it's pretty easy. The challenge we face is handling the *volume* of activities we now know are critical to successful relationship marketing.

We need to look for leverage.

WHAT IS LEVERAGE?

When we're talking about leverage, we're talking about increasing the amount of total output we can yield within a fixed amount of time. Sending five e-mails in the time that it used to take to send one is gaining leverage over our investment of time.

Why Is Leverage So Important?

Recall our earlier focus on Consistency (the C in CAPITAL). In order to act consistently, we need a reliable trigger, the actions, and a good reward for our actions. The less work the action requires, the more likely we are to repeat that action, building habit.

Now that you understand the full relationship marketing process (CAPITA), the last step, Leverage, is about making it easier to accomplish everything before it. And it connects back to the beginning (Consistency), as the more leverage we have, the more consistent we are.

Consider this chapter the upper-level elective in relationship marketing. You may not need it to accomplish your goals, but it sure will help. You'll also be best served by having a good grasp of the prerequisite chapters, as we're building on everything we've covered so far.

We've already been talking about gaining leverage throughout the book. In fact, if we were to fix our North Star on what we're trying to achieve, it would be on how to effectively use your time in order to ring that bell.

- Using an automated database instead of manually updating a spreadsheet (or worse, yet, trying to keep track of everything in your head) gives us more leverage.

- Narrowing down the number of people we engage with to those most likely to add value gives us more leverage over our time that could have been wasted on lower priority relationships.

These are just two examples.

Being Measured in Your Level of Investment

If you ever find yourself facing so much internal resistance to accomplishing a task, the solution isn't to skip the task, it's to do less of the task itself. Lightening our load ensures that we get something done and continue building up that habit. Once we get that repetitive engine humming, then we can slowly increase the load. If it starts to sputter, then we ease off to ensure we don't stall out.

In his *Tiny Habits* program, B.J. Fogg urges to build a new habit by associating it to something we already do, and this habit should be so tiny—like flossing a single tooth—that you'll face no resistance to actually doing it. How do we apply this concept to relationship marketing?

Limiting the Number of People You Need to Proactively Keep in Your Sphere

This goes back to the addition by subtraction concept. The fewer people we need to engage with on a daily basis, the better.

This is usually best done at the bucket level. Working top down, consider the number of people in the bucket. Do they all need to be there? Could we split the bucket into two (higher and lower priority)?

One of the easiest ways to gain leverage while still delivering on the outcome is by adjusting the cadence at which you need to engage with your sphere. Unless there is an immediate action on the horizon that requires your urgent engagement (such as a client considering your proposal, or being actively in-market now), people probably won't even notice that you're engaging with them every 45 days instead of every 30—and you just cut down your amount of work by 33 percent!

Limiting Your Level of Investment in a Certain Tier or Person

One of my underlying flaws is the desire to please and to be appreciated. So when I am reaching out to someone, I want to go the extra mile, be invaluable, be the person's best friend.

Well, I can't do that for everyone.

In Prioritization, we talked about creating tiers in our sphere of influence, based on the perceived amount of value we can hope a particular set of relationships will yield. In Adding Value, we connected the amount of value we hope to yield with the amount of resources we put into increasing our perceived value in those people's eyes.

I'm going to reemphasize that last point and remind you to spend *more* energy on your higher-priority relationships and less energy on your lower-priority relationships. That means your top past clients get a personal invite to dinner once a quarter, and cold leads get a monthly newsletter. *We must resist the urge to treat everyone homogeneously.*

Your *investment* in a relationship is also a function of two factors: the amount of *time* applied and the quantity of *resources*— usually money—required in order to build mindshare. What are you trying to optimize for? What will make a bigger impact on that particular person?

A personalized e-mail costs nothing but can take up a substantial amount of time. Texting your virtual assistant to "buy Nancy a gift" takes you no time, but the cost of the gift plus your VA's time to orchestrate it all may cause you to think twice.

There is no clear solution here, other than to enter every interaction with the intention of matching the level of effort applied with the amount of value you hope to one day accrue.

There is, however, one clear path to reducing the amount of time it takes when Adding Value.

TEMPLATIZING YOUR ACTIONS

If there are actions we repeatedly take in our relationship marketing initiatives, by templatizing them as much as possible, we can reduce the amount of time, resources, and effort to execute repeatedly.

Let's start with e-mail templates—a clear quick win. Even the e-mail signature, nearly universal to every mail client, is itself a template. Imagine having to write all your contact information and uploading that microscopic company logo *every time you sent a message*. Savagery.

Your database should be able to support e-mail templates. Some have more capabilities than others. If not, hopefully your mail client does. There are also third-party tools that one can use, such as TextExpander. You'll find them in Appendix A.

The point here is not necessarily to template the *full* message so you don't have to write a word. That may be the solution in some cases, likely for lower-priority relationships in which one would not invest much personal effort. We're simply trying to reduce the repetitive action—what we would say *no matter who the recipient was*. It is on us, at the time of sending the message, to make the necessary customizations. Instead of writing the e-mail from scratch, we can drop in a template, recall any notes, past conversations, or other intelligence we've accrued, and make those small customizations.

Templates should not be limited to e-mail, however.

- Are there certain text messages you send often? Your database's mobile client may have text message templates. If not, your smartphone likely supports that.

- Keep a list of links to books handy so you can easily pick a book to send to someone.

- Buy a stack of gift cards and have them ready to go in stamped envelopes with return addresses and a blank card so you can quickly write a personal message, add a mailing address, and drop a card into your nearest mail box.

- Pick out one or two spots for coffee or meals in town so you (or your VA) don't have to find a place each time you have a meeting.

There are additional benefits to having templated actions coded into our interface. Yes, it can be used to save time. Preloading templates for new users, as well as allowing teammates and employees to share content with each other, helps ensure some level of consistency, best-practice sharing, and reducing the adoption curve. One could even go as far as creating a number of e-mail templates in your voice, and then handing them off to your virtual assistant to reach out personally on your behalf.

It also changes how we approach *how we add value.* You want to follow up with someone, but you're facing a blank e-mail editor, with no idea what to say. By having precoded templates, "what do I say?" turns into the much easier "which message do I send?"

The aim is to reduce the amount of effort one has to exert without a major reduction in the value delivered to that relationship. If the e-mail template takes the form of a normal e-mail I would write, is coded to automatically insert personalized information (first name is obvious, but maybe even "I know we spoke back in *July*") and some other personal note ("BTW, how's Rover doing? I know he was sick last time we spoke."), our recipient perceives and therefore receives the value of a personal communication. Unbeknownst to them, I did it in a quarter of the time that one would normally expect. Our aim is to maximize the value delivered while reducing the cost to us.

For a plethora of e-mail templates, see Appendix C, or visit our digital appendix.

USING PRESTRUCTURED RECIPES

Templates don't need to be limited to a single action. If there are a series of actions that are executed consistently for a certain type of relationship or for a certain event, then stringing them together into a "Program," "Automation," or "Campaign" (the verbiage alters depending on the tool you might be using) can help you execute effectively. The individual messages (or other actions) can be triggered to go off at specified intervals.

The most popular form of this is the "drip marketing campaign," a series of e-mails that automatically go out, usually without any intervention from the sender. While these are programmed to "drip on someone" until people give up and respond to you, these can also be executed independent of any other actions.

This is not limited to e-mails. Theoretically, any action—automated or not— can be inserted into a sequence. These include:

- Adding a contact as a friend on a social network

- Giving them a call

- Stopping by their office

- Buying a gift

- Doing research

- Updating their status in your system

- And virtually anything else

It doesn't have to be an action that is executed without our intervention, although that's possible, too.

> ### The real beauty happens when *people* and *technology* work hand-in-hand.

Birthday reminders are obvious. But if your system is programmed to alert you on a particular personal or professional anniversary of a contact, you can either automatically send a message or have the system set a reminder for your dashboard that day to call or text the person.

What we're doing here is disassociating the *strategy* of determining what to do with the *execution* of the prescribed actions. We can put a ton of thought and creativity into devising the right strategy to take in a particular sequence. Day to day, we can mindlessly execute the individual actions our system is saying are due.

One of the other powerful components here is the ability for these programs to operate on a potentially infinite timescale, just as the cadence settings in your database could remind you to stay in touch once a quarter until one of you is six feet under (and maybe a little bit beyond that). One example I use is for when people change jobs. If I notice a new job, I'll drop the contact into a new job program. It's common, if not expected, in the present day to congratulate someone on a new job title. LinkedIn has lubricated that flow so much that all you need to do is a click a button on a push notification to send congratulations, thereby decreasing the value. But what if you had a program that sent an e-mail one month after ("How was the first month?"), told you to call them a year after ("Wow, you made it a year!"), even five years later ("Five years? You must be CEO by now!")? Your database, combined with the process that you outline for it, can be the elephant that never forgets. If your campaigns are giving you valuable actions that you had *no idea about* before, then it's working!

We can start to see the building blocks of powerful systems form. Imagine if, as a real estate agent, new Internet leads are automatically uploaded to your database. Those leads instantly go into a category of your database. Your database is smart enough to know that whenever a new contact is added to that category, it will automatically kick off a series of e-mail templates that *look* personal. If the person responds, that goes directly to you, ending the sequence. Otherwise, at some point in the campaign, the system prescribes an action for you to take, telling you to call the person. You didn't even know that lead existed until that e-mail response came in, or your dashboard told you to call someone. Either way, your database already has everything there is to know on that person, allowing you to quickly build a personal relationship.

When we talked about Adding Value, we brought up the idea of standing out. One way of standing out is shifting your message over time. We gave the specific example of engaging people periodically after they announce job changes, as a tool to maintain cadence while simultaneously standing out from the noise of congratulatory likes and comments enabled by social platforms.

Here's what it would look like if you programmed a campaign to kick off whenever you notice someone changing jobs:

- Wait 5 days, then send them my predefined "Congratulations on your new job!" e-mail.

- Wait 25 days, then send them my predefined "Checking in on new job" e-mail.

- Wait 30 days, then send me a reminder to research possible introductions at the company.

- At the same time, send me a reminder to research any possible business opportunities.

- Wait 12 months, then send them my predefined "Happy one year!" e-mail.

See? You can break down what would normally be a fair amount of work into something you write once and execute many times.
    Some other quick ideas:

- When people buy a new house, send them a number of new homeowner tips, such as reminding them to check their air filter or prep for the winter.

- When people have a child, send them periodic "checking in" e-mails along with helpful parenting tips.

- After you meet people at a conference, send them a series of e-mails with resources and more information about yourself, etc.

- If you just finished a client project, or someone becomes a customer, have a program that sends messages saying thank you, checking in later, asking for reviews, asking for an introduction, etc.

- If people are a potential hire, every six months send them one of a number of e-mails, asking if they are in the market, or what they'd be looking for next.

See sample templates in Appendix C.

A WARNING ABOUT AUTOMATION

There was a short window in the early 2000s when autoresponders were all the rage. You e-mail an address, and you instantly receive a response. It used to be for "information you were requesting."

Now it's usually for "I'm on vacation, but probably still checking my e-mail" or the holier-than-thou "I'm super busy so I'm going to take a while to respond to you, if at all."

That's not the automation we're trying to achieve here. Going back to the idea of leverage, we're trying to reduce the amount of effort we have to exert in order to deliver value to a relationship.

We've already talked about some of the building blocks of automation, templating actions or stringing a series of actions into a program. We could go one step further and have these messages or programs go off without us doing anything.

I'm actually going to warn you *against* going the automation route. At least not yet. Overautomation runs the risk of errors, such as the wrong person getting the wrong message, making them realize that they aren't important enough to you to warrant a truly personal outreach.

Your sphere should be completely oblivious to any mechanization of your relationship marketing efforts.

There is a hybrid approach that is encapsulated in programs or templates. Instead of taking the action unassisted, it can prompt you, with the message cued up and ready to go. You have to hit Send, leaving it up to you to review the message, make any changes, ignore the action, or click Send. The templates and programs that we provide require human intervention at every step.

Once you have built up trust in the system you've implemented, it should be an easy tweak to have the actions, to the greatest extent possible, be dispatched without your intervention.

SHAY HATA, REALTOR

Tactically, we implement processes that help us ensure that, at the right time, we're holding their hand and they hear from us every day. We are heavy users of our database's (we use Contactually) programs and functionality, which helps us reach out at the right time. For example, amid the usual roller coaster of emotions that accompanies the closing process of buying a home, we automatically e-mail them, reminding them to call the gas/electric/Internet companies, and we provide a recommendation for a locksmith.

REACHING OUT BASED ON ARTIFICIAL INTELLIGENCE

I'm writing this book in 2018 as we are just starting to see the crest of the data wave. We can hop on our surfboards and leverage the data-driven tools at our fingertips to help our businesses and careers thrive. It's an incredibly exciting time because new technologies are rolling out monthly that have the potential to completely change how we understand the world.

With mass amounts of data being collected, low-cost computing power to process it, and generations of developers providing the building blocks that can be connected together in the right way to create experiences, why wouldn't we use these tools in our relationship building? Using the right tools can be like throwing a can of lighter fluid onto a fire. When used properly, the right tools can amplify you. Improperly applied, they can blow up your house.

Here are a few examples, starting with the most basic:

You have a monthly newsletter that, in addition to your one-on-one messages, has *pixel tracking* turned on, so your mail server is notified whenever your message is opened. Through that, you can also identify interesting trends. Of the 3,000 people on your monthly newsletter, you can identify who is opening it, who is opening it *multiple times*, and who is opening *most of your messages*. Those are the people you choose to reach out to one-on-one, as they are the ones who clearly are expressing some interest in hearing what you have to say.

In your normal e-mail message, you include a few links to certain pages on your website. Your website has some tracking built in, so from the link in the e-mail, it knows who the person is. It can not only detect that the person came from an e-mail, but records as the person browses your site, disappears, then reappears on your site a few months later looking at a particular page. When it sees an increase in activity, it sends a short notification to your phone, telling you what articles or listings are attracting most of the attention. So even if people aren't responding to an e-mail from you, you give them a call, recommending content from your site, without them knowing that those recommendations came directly from them.

You've amassed an enormous database of relationships after years of client projects, referrals, and gallons of coffee. You have your key relationships prioritized; however, there is still a massive pool of people you just aren't sure what to do with. No problem. You can subscribe to a service that plugs right into your database, extracts the relevant information for each contact, and then compares that list to its own database on every consumer and professional in the world. But that database is plugged into an even bigger stream of well-anonymized data, going out to data sources that can provide credit history, web browsing history, demographic information, social media posts. It won't give you that information directly, but what it *can* do is even more powerful, as this tool leverages *predictive analytics*, which looks at past patterns and activities to give some likelihood of an event happening. If it sees a pattern in what homebuyers do six to nine months before a move, and it sees the same pattern for a few people in your database, it can give you an informed guess that those relationships are going to move soon, *whether or not they know it*. It may be hard to wrap your head around, but you don't need to know the inner workings, as long as you know that the system is right most of the time. It helps narrow the long tail of your database—thousands of contacts, to a smaller subset.

These kinds of technologies previously were only available to major marketing organizations that were willing to throw hundreds of thousands of dollars at vendors, buy terabytes of data, and spend years iterating, sometimes embarrassing themselves in the process.[1]

Exciting times.

What matters is that your intent of maintaining a personal and authentic relationship is only *aided*, not *driven*, by technology.

I've included a few examples in Appendix A of products that can help you leverage data in the right way.

USING A
VIRTUAL ASSISTANT

If you can afford it, I can't recommend enough having an in-house or virtual assistant to help with your relationship marketing abilities.

Reducing task completion friction should be a focus of your setup, so you can quickly translate "I want to do this" to "done." And what better way to do that, beyond having effective tools and templates, than to delegate that to someone else?

A virtual assistant, or "engagement manager," can help with your relationship marketing efforts in numerous ways, while still allowing you to be the actual face of the relationship.

What specific relationship marketing tasks could a virtual or other assistant offer?

- Prioritizing relationships

- Sending out larger communications (you simply give rough points of what you want to get across)

- Translating raw notes and meeting debriefs into well-stored notes and actions

- Handling incoming correspondence, especially weeding out low-priority tasks

- Operating consistently, prompting you to do the same and be more in reactive mode

Some people may go even further and rely on a virtual assistant to manage all relationship activities for them. I advise against it because it risks inauthentic communications. Imagine if your VA had been keeping up with someone for years, but you couldn't remember a single element of "your" discussions with the person when you run into each other at an event?

PATRICK EWERS, EXECUTIVE AND RELATIONSHIP MARKETING COACH

At the end of the day, you can only hack your own time and productivity so far before hitting a wall. When that inevitably happens, you need to be prepared to scale with a resource outside yourself.

So here's a counterintuitive question: How could you work with a virtual assistant to help you manage your relationships? The question might seem odd at first, but think about it: at some point, nearly every other aspect of successful business management is eventually (at least partially) delegated.

Why *not* relationship management?

To answer that question, I'd like to introduce the concept of an Engagement Manager (EM), a unique spin on a traditional virtual assistant focused on enabling you to deliver better experiences to your network at scale.

Let me give you a pragmatic example you can roll out immediately (if you already have an assistant): Would you agree it's a good idea to send a follow-up e-mail after every meeting you have? Most people would, yet people admit they only do so about 50 percent of the time (at best).

Why? Because a truly meaningful, valuable follow-up email can take 10 to 15 minutes to write, and they simply don't have the time. With an EM, that investment could be reduced to a minute. Let me explain.

Immediately following a meeting, pull out your phone and spend 30 seconds dictating the rough outline of a follow-up e-mail. Your EM would receive that, turn it into an e-mail that reads well, and place it in your drafts folder for review.

Now, at the end of an eight-meeting day, all you have to do is spend two or three minutes reviewing and sending eight prewritten e-mails sitting in your drafts folder. That's it. Simple though it may be, I've seen this tactic alone save up to an hour a day.

I truly believe working with a resource like an EM is one of the most valuable investments you can make, as they can give you the leverage you need to deliver great experiences at scale.

GETTING TACTICAL

Here is how we can increase the likelihood that we'll act consistently to add value and stay engaged with our sphere:

- Identify the actions that you are doing, or plan to do, repeatedly.

- Of those actions, what can be templated? Many e-mails or text messages can be.

- Identify which set of actions can be put together in a sequence that can be preprogrammed for you in your database or marketing system.

- If at all possible, delegate actions that you don't need to do personally to a virtual assistant.

QUICK WIN

Create three e-mail templates that you believe you would use often, and put them in your e-mail client, or at least in a note tool. Recommended templates: check in, introduction, and thank you e-mails.

KEY TAKEAWAYS

- Look for ways to reduce the amount of effort without sacrificing your goal.

- Gain more leverage by ensuring you are focused on your most valuable relationships, or better balancing the amount of effort you exert.

- Templatizing individual or series of actions help you execute repeatedly.

- Automation can help, but only do it when you're ready.

- A third party can help lighten your load.

CHAPTER

13

GETTING RESULTS

Everyone looks to invest in their sphere of influence for different reasons. While the outputs may vary from person to person, the important thing is that there *is* an output.

If you do not see a return on your investment, the opportunity cost of your investment will rear its ugly head. What are you *not* spending time, money, or other resources on that you could be? Are all of these coffee meetings, e-mails, phone calls, and papercuts while packing your handmade origami gifts really worth it?

The great author, salesman, and quote machine Zig Ziglar (whose stage name is definitely much catchier than his birth name, Hilary Hinton Ziglar), was known for saying, *"You will get all you want in life, if you help enough other people get what they want."* While that's a core tenet of this book, especially the chapter on adding value, this admittedly can be a bit frustrating. What if *all you want* is to get 10 referrals? What if *all you want* is a 90 percent client retention rate? How do you get that?

You can't. Anyone who tells you that they have *the* solution proven to translate a specific set of actions into a specific set of outputs is selling you a bill of goods.

The challenge we face is that there is no guarantee of results from any one action. *Building a relationship and demonstrating value may or may not generate a return*. If the value you receive is indeterminate, it's further unclear what actions are most proven to generate value. While this may be the case, I truly believe that the foundation of successful relationship marketing is to have a giver's mentality.

In this chapter, there are two noteworthy points I want to relay to you:

- It is absolutely worth being proactive to try to solicit the returns you are asking for.

- Track the results of efforts at different levels.

To start off, we are going to tackle the hardest, yet most important part of relationship marketing. How do you maximize the opportunities generated from your prior investment?

MAKING THE ASK . . . OR DO YOU?

What type of person are you? Are you direct, even somewhat aggressive, and is that what you and your clientele respond to? Or are you more passive, just ensuring that they consider you if and when there is an opportunity to work together?

Be Direct

Being fearful about making the ask is not uncommon. A good way around it is to consider scripting the response.

Be Clear

We spend our days in a reality distortion field.[1] We know the intimate details about how our industry operates, how transactions happen, what's important and not important, and what we value. Because we're in the thick of it all day long, we may make the false assumption that the outside world knows that, too. *If people aren't in the same business as you, they don't know how you do business.* You have to educate those around you on what would be most valuable to you. It's simple. Make it clear.

Have your ask ready. How many times have you been asked, whether virtually or in person, *how can I help you?* It's a basic, open, and generous question through which someone is making you a hopefully genuine offer. Yet most people *completely* fumble the answer. Preparing a scripted response can help. The more specific, the better.

"I'm looking to meet couples who recently had their first child and are still living in an apartment."

"I would appreciate a referral to anyone who is starting their own business and wants some guidance on navigating all the local laws."

"If you know anyone who is considering moving to the Austin area, I'm happy to be a resource on what neighborhoods to consider."

Do they know how to reach you? You may think this is cheesy, but I think the e-mail signature is one of the most underutilized tools out there. Have you added your contact information to your personal bio?

DEREK COBURN, WEALTH MANAGER AND COFOUNDER OF CADRE

Do people know what you do? Sometimes we just need to make it clear what we do. Five or so years ago, as a way to differentiate myself as a financial advisor, I was marketing myself as a personal CFO. I thought it sounded better than a financial advisor. I had clients that rallied around it. I had clients who were introducing me to other people saying, "I have a personal CFO who's doing so much more for me than just overseeing my financial planning."

I had a conversation with a good friend from college who had received an inheritance, and we were talking about what I do, and he said, "Wow, I thought you were a personal CFO. I didn't realize that you managed money. I went out and hired a different financial advisor. If I would have known what you did, I would have worked with you."

I'm probably not going to be the right solution for somebody unless they have seven figures of investable assets. If they don't fit that profile, I may not mention it at all, as I don't want to have to turn down a friend. Otherwise, I keep it simple and nonconfrontational: "Hey, I own a wealth management firm and we do a lot of things to help people manage their money." If I'm being really casual about it, "We do a lot of things to help people manage their money, and if you ever need any help or have any questions with your investment planning, your insurance planning, your estate planning, I'd be happy to be a sounding board for you." I'm not forcing them to sit down with me, or have to say yes or no. I'm just making sure they know that I am available to help them.

I think a lot of professionals agree to work with their friends because they want to make sure they are taken care of. This is fine unless your friend has needs that are outside of what you typically provide. For example, I have a minimum account size for my wealth management business. If I have a friend below that threshold who's in need of advice, I may be tempted to work with them as a favor. However, this will blow up the majority of the time because my business isn't set up to support small clients. What I do in these scenarios is recommend another option and offer to review the advice they are getting. Unless someone has a need that matches what I deliver, it's not worth risking the friendship.

As you wrap up every interaction, do you think you can share your ask? It doesn't have to be a direct ask. It could be a reminder to them of what is important to you, and if they desire to help you, what would be most valuable. It doesn't have to be formal. A casual "Oh, by the way, if you know any developers that do X, let me know" is a simple and easy ask at the end of a conversation.

There is no wrong way about it. As long as you are seeking a solution to the question, "Does my tribe know what would be most valuable to me?"

MICHAEL MARGOLIS, FOUNDER OF STORIED

Margolis offers unique expertise on how to tell the story of disruptive innovation. With such a niche focus, most of his business has come via long-term relationships with clients and prospects.

How much does your sphere really know you?

A few years back, I went traveling for 500 days as an executive nomad, teaching around the world, and living in hotels with two carry-on bags. My travels took me to four continents and 12 countries, including India and Australia. When I came back to the States, I realized people in my sphere would get a little glimpse of my life and what I'm up to through social media, but they don't really know the whole story.

We have so many demands for our attention. Everyone wants to meet for coffee. To be able to crack that noise, you have to establish relevance. Create a pattern interrupt.

A pattern interrupt is what makes you stand out, and often what makes people think, "That's the company I want to keep."

Social media is definitely part of the conversation, but I realized I was only engaging in one-way communication.

> In order to complete the circuit, I needed to ensure that the people who were seeing my posts were also engaging with me directly.
>
> There were so many people in my network I hadn't talked to, so now I spend an hour a day catching up with customers, around 15 minutes apiece. It was an absolute game-changer for my opportunity pipeline.

Be Top of Mind When They're Making Decisions

A few years into Contactually, we thought there might be an opportunity to provide our platform to major brands. None of us had any business development experience, so we sought to do what we know best, build relationships. By attending the right conferences, gaining introductions, and lots of casual conversations, we were able to reach the right people. Success, right? Not so fast. The bigger the organization, the slower and more thoughtful they often are when it comes to technology decisions, especially something as pivotal as CRM.

I am thankful to have a number of more experienced leaders as mentors. One of them casually shared his tactic for business development. Your job, when it comes to generating new business, is to ensure that you have enough mindshare that, when an opportunity arises on a client's end, independent of outside influences, they think of you.

Normal sales canon rejects this. If they aren't actively in purchasing mode, an account executive puts them into Closed/Lost status, and hopefully remembers to put them on a nurture campaign and follow up in six months. If we are truly looking to build a relationship, we need to *abandon any timelines, and just ensure we are there when they are ready to move forward*.

In many cases, it's helpful to be direct in your time-independent offer. Consumers and decision makers are constantly being bombarded with "buy now" calls to action. So to have someone *not* expecting you're in buy mode, and just care about building a relationship for an eventual transaction, will set you apart and achieve exactly what you're trying to do: establish a connection in the hopes that, some day in the future, they will be in buy mode. When I was raising our first round of venture capital, I was given similar advice: *the best way to raise money is to meet when you aren't raising.*

Try this, almost word for word:

> I'm just looking to build a relationship with you, in the hopes that we can work together, be it in six months or six years. I'm here for the long term.

You will elicit a very different reaction than your previous encounters.

JOHN CORCORAN, COFOUNDER OF RISE25

John Corcoran is one of the best connectors I know—working with entrepreneurs of all types and helping them turn relationships into revenue.

Lowell Weiss was a White House speechwriter. When I was an intern in the White House speechwriting office in the fall of 1997, alongside thousands of other interns, I got along with him really well. Super nice guy, down to earth. He'd been in journalism, and actually ghost authored James Carville's first book, *We're Right, They're Wrong: A Handbook for Spirited Progressives*, which is how he got the job in the White House. He was pinching himself that he'd gone from *Atlantic Weekly* to writing for James Carville to the White House. He was a younger guy, too, so he related with me really well.

I did everything I could to maintain that relationship, and to deliver as much value to him as possible. Starting with, of course, while I was there interning, going over and above delivering research and things that he needed, and trying to do it as fast as possible and as high quality as possible. After I completed the internship during the fall quarter of my senior year, I went back to college because I hadn't graduated yet. And while I was back in college, I was still thinking of him. I was reading articles in the newspaper, seeing passages of literature, and then snipping these things out and sending them to him from time to time. Not as a way of saying, "Hey, got a job for me?" but as saying, "Hey, this is something that I think would make your life easier. I think you might be able to incorporate this into a speech you are working on." Sure enough, a year and a half later, I get a call out of the blue. He knew I was interested in coming back and getting a job at the White House. But I was also one of thousands of former interns. Most never get a job afterward.

He calls me up and says, "Hey, I heard about this job as a writer." I'm 23 years old. I have a B.A. in English from a party school. He calls me up, tells me about it, and says, "I'm going to pass your name along to the person who's hiring for it, and she's going to give you a call." Sure enough, a couple of days later, she gives me a call, and the rest is history. That's how I got that job. That's just one example. I did not have a degree from an Ivy League school or connections to wealthy donors.

Ask for a Seat at the Table

We often find ourselves in competitive situations. You are not the only real estate agent. You're not the only accountant. There are other software companies they can choose to work with.

Try this. When speaking with someone with whom you hope to eventually work, just drop the following:

> I know you may not be looking to make a decision yet. All I ask is that when you start evaluating your options, I have the opportunity to share what we do and how we work.

What you're doing is giving the power back to your contact. You're not forcing a decision on people right now. Rather, you're attaching yourself to any future decisions they may make. This relates back to one of our points about adding value, the NNTR, or No Need To Reply. You're not creating more work and stress for them. You're simply bookmarking yourself on the "list of people to talk to when moving forward." That's all you were aiming for, right?

CONTROL AND TRACK
WHAT YOU CAN

You can be as passive or as proactive as you feel fits your personality or the timeliness and importance of the ask itself. The key underlying point is that there are no guaranteed results.

A traditional sales organization relies on running its process enough times that patterns emerge. From patterns, metrics come to the surface that can be tied back to revenue. If business leaders know which and how many activities resulted in each sale made, they can do the math to understand how to scale. If we know that a prospect will pick up the phone 30 percent of the time, and of those who talk to us, 25 percent will end up converting to customers, then for every 200 dials made, we'll get 14 sales. I'm making wild assumptions here, but you can see the logic in thinking that they can simply increase the amount of activities and see the dollar bills flowing in and a commensurate rate. Business!

A true sales organization isn't as clean as that, and relationship marketing is far less so. For one, it's highly unlikely that we are operating at the statistical significance (i.e., doing the thousands of calls, e-mails, and other activities) that would give us any kind of confidence in our numbers. Also, we are building long-lasting relationships with indeterminate timelines and activities, not "dialing for dollars." When our company was nothing more than a few months old, a little bit of angel investment, and a half-working prototype, we brought on our first salesperson. In hindsight, it was extremely premature. He had been incredibly impactful for a couple of our advisors' organizations, so we were warned that the only issue we would face would be handling the volume of sales he would generate. He lasted six weeks and made zero sales. Not even a decent opportunity created. His sole line at daily check-ins, "just dialing for dollars today," is forever seared in my brain.

Remember, what we're doing in relationship marketing is ensuring that we continue to maintain a strong bond between a prospective partner and ourselves. There are dump trucks full of reasons why they may not go with you, which I'll lay out here:

- As much as they liked you, there was someone else they had a closer relationship with. If they didn't hire their nephew, Thanksgiving dinner would be even more awkward.

- While you were following up consistently, someone else just happened to hit the nail on the head; right time, right place.

- They were mistaken as to your expertise; they didn't realize that while your core line of business was condos downtown, you could also handle McMansions out in the suburbs.

- They simply are not in the mode to make another transaction, nor do they know anyone in their sphere of influence who is.

And all of those are OK, and completely understandable. A fundamental nuance of relationship marketing is to build relationships on the *likelihood, not certainty* that they would work with you again. Therefore, the key underlying point to convey is you cannot control the results you will achieve. All you can control are the actions that you will take.

> You have power over your mind—not outside events. Realize this, and you will find strength.
> —MARCUS AURELIUS

Pay attention to the actions that you take and the direct response to those actions.

TRACKING LEADING INDICATORS

You're zipping down the highway, turning your morning commute into the epic car chase scene in the 1998 Robert De Niro movie *Ronin*. While you're swerving around yet another tractor-trailer, you notice that your instrument panel is flashing a yellow indicator. Purely by process of elimination, you realize this is warning you that one or more of your tires has low tire pressure.

Leading indicators are measurements or signals that foretell a likely result. Your car is telling you that you have a problem that, if not addressed, could result in a potentially catastrophic event. In our sales example earlier in the chapter, the rate at which your phone calls are getting answered is a leading indicator of the number of sales you'll be making. Leading indicators are a useful tool when the desired result will not manifest for long periods of time, if at all.

How can we apply leading indicators in the work that we do?

The leading indicators should revolve around the exact actions that we take, and the immediate response to them.

What Actions Are We Taking?

The blessing in this era is that nearly everything *can* be tracked, so our activities can be quantified. We can easily count the number of messages sent, calls made, meetings held. The curse, therefore, is that, in order to derive a leading indicator of performance, we *should* be aggregating and analyzing that information.

Luckily, this is where your database or relationship marketing tool(s) can win the day.

Your system should be able to answer the following questions for you, your team, or organization:

- How many touches are we making in a given period?

- How many people are we engaging with?

- How many meetings have I had?
- At what frequency am I engaging with my relationships?
- What channels am I using?
- What templates or preset actions am I using?
- How many people are in my buckets?

How Do Those Actions Match up Against the Goals I've Set?

We introduced the CAPITAL strategy by identifying what our overlying goals are. Those were our high-level goals, so in order to break it down, we prioritized our sphere, and then laid out what timely engagement looked like for those key people. The arithmetic is simple:

(# of people you want to engage with) × (# of times you need to engage them in a given year) = # of engagements you need to have, at minimum

Once you have that number, you can easily see what your short-term goal is. Let's say that you had 250 people in your sphere of influence with whom you wanted to speak to at least once a quarter. That's 1,000 touches in a year, at most. That equates to engaging with about 19 people a week, or four people a day. Great, now you can set that goal very clearly.

Track the overall activity you wish to achieve. You tell yourself that you want to engage with 19 of your contacts once a week and have your database monitor it for you. As you grind through the week, how are you tracking to that objective?

Track the perceived health of your relationships. Engineers and data scientists spend a considerable amount of time predicting the bidirectional health of our professional relationships. The raw signal that we *can*, with absolute certainty, measure is the frequency with which we are engaging relative to the goal that we set.

An early innovation we made was investing in the concept of *gamification*, the act of taking psychological mechanics that make games so fun and engaging and applying it to something else to encourage similar behavior. You know that when you see green, that usually means good, while red is a negative indicator. So if a database shows a contact with a green indicator, that's the sign of a healthy relationship, whereas red should compel you to identify a problem, pushing you to fix it. Another way, which could be crudely programmed into a formula in a spreadsheet, is to aggregate those results.

You have 250 contacts, and you want to follow up with them every 90 days. On average, you're engaging with half within the desired interval, and the other half don't get as frequent engagement. A simple formula would indicate you're achieving 50 percent of your goal. If you were assigned a letter grade for getting a 50 out of 100, congrats, it's like your teacher drew a big fat F on your report card.

The simple question you should be asking yourself as you think about a leading indicator is, am I doing the activities that I committed to doing?

What Is the Immediate Response to My Actions?

You cannot control the actions of others, but you can definitely observe and track them.

- We don't necessarily know if the e-mail we sent is going to generate a referral weeks or months later, but did the recipient at least open the message?
- Did recipients acknowledge the gift you sent them with a thank you note?
- Did they click on the link you sent them?

The golfer who, not having the catlike eyesight to identify exactly where the ball landed, can at least identify if his swing made a satisfactory *thwap*, and see the initial arc and direction to know if he'll be the buying beers for everyone at the clubhouse later.

Best-in-class marketing systems will automate as much of these results as possible—open, click, and reply tracking is no longer a dark art. Tracking some of the other activities, like whether or not a contact replied to a social media post or thanked you, might require a little bit of manual work. Put together, this will provide a *leading indicator* to show that you're at least on the right path.

You can also compare this to your past performance, that of your peers, or the industry in general. For instance, if you want to benchmark your performance to the industry, Mailchimp notes that messaging campaigns for the consulting industry net on average a 19.5 percent open rate and a 2.26 percent click rate.[2] Granted, this is for mass-marketing tools like e-mail newsletters and impersonal drip campaigns. You can, however, use this as a baseline of comparison, and if your personal outreaches perform at a lower rate, then it should warrant some deeper diagnostics. Are your messages coming across as impersonal or uninteresting?

TRACKING WHAT DOES AND DOESN'T WORK

Death, taxes, *and change* are the only guarantees in life. If we are ever to improve, not only do we have to act consistently, we have to iterate on our methods to better understand what works.

> *External things are not the problem. It's your assessment of them. Which you can erase right now.*
> —MARCUS AURELIUS

The concept of test-learn-iterate is likely not a foreign concept. Everything we do has the potential to be a test, where we learn from the results, and iterate from there. One of the additional benefits of having so much data available to us is the ability to measure the performance of our actions *relative to other actions*.

What channels are getting the best engagement rate? Do I seem to get better responses when I'm texting people? Or is e-mail still the universal way to engage with someone?

What messages are getting the best responses? Does one subject line work better than another? Do I get more clicks if I include the raw link or use a few words in a sentence as a hyperlink?

One could go so far as to implement A/B testing, in which half an audience receives one version of a message, and the other half receives a slight variation. By doing that, and keeping everything else the same, you have the ability to compare the results to determine which performs better. This is a staple of digital marketing organizations and, with some thought, this can be tracked as well. Even at a basic level, you could simply have two e-mail templates, and everyone with a last name A-M gets one version, and N-Z another. Then just track what percentage of each e-mail gets a response. Yes, a lot of work, but as we talked about in leverage, that's where investing in the right tooling (e.g., a database) should help.

Tracking Outcomes and Celebrating the Wins

If the ultimate goal of relationship marketing is to generate an outcome, then you better believe that, for all the work we put into it, we want to be aware of what related or unrelated outcomes are occurring. That should further reinforce our habits. When you get an opportunity, however or wherever it comes from, it is important to make sure that you put one more in the "win" column.

Remember those who provided you with some kind of opportunity, for those are the people who will likely do it again for you. A source (or sources) of an outcome you were seeking should, without question, be clearly identified. In an earlier chapter, we shared that those who have already made a referral are far more likely to provide one than those who didn't. So when receiving a new opportunity, not only do you want to record the opportunity but who it is from. Move them to a higher-priority bucket and kick off a *thank you* program that triggers a series of actions, using this as material for a future follow-up.

It's about the opportunity, not the outcome. One small clarifying point. From your network, are you seeking more sales? Or more *opportunities*? Are you solely looking for the outcome, or just the *at-bats?* Yes, there is no question you ultimately desire the latter. Repeat after me: *my sphere is here to give me more opportunities.* Sales are not guaranteed—that's on you.

Part of my charter as CEO is industry relations. I have had the opportunity to, without any particular opportunity in sight, build personal and authentic relationships with a variety of influential people in numerous industries. Some are consultants who work with our target market. We've been careful in meeting with them under the auspices of genuine care. It's far too easy to engage in these conversations with false pretenses, only to fish for opportunities. We meet with them because we care about the industry and want to ensure that we are doing what we can to help them be successful, even if it's as simple as reposting an article they share. While I desire to be authentic and genuine, when we are discussing our near-term sales prospects and activities to bring in new customers, there's inevitably some internal pushback—was that worth it?

Yet some of our biggest sales have come not from asking or cold calls or pitches but from a completely unprompted e-mail introduction at 5 p.m. on a Thursday. You'd better believe that the introduction quickly elevated them to a champion in my database.

That leads me to my last, and maybe most important point. The results will not always be clear. Let me repeat that.

THE RESULTS WILL NOT ALWAYS BE CLEAR

We have to gain comfort with the grayness and uncertainty of connecting our actions to outcomes. We're not always going to be sure which investments with which people lead to the desired opportunities, nor will we be able, with complete certainty, to connect an opportunity received with a decision we made at some point in time. The best we can do is *try* to measure it.

> Half the money I spend on advertising is wasted;
> the trouble is I don't know which half.
> **—JOHN WANAMAKER**

We're not alone. In the marketing world, *attribution*—connecting a marketing campaign to a sale—is a major challenge, both online and offline. We have invested an immense amount of time into tracking where every potential customer came from. *Multitouch attribution* takes it even further, where one tries to understand what series of touchpoints led to a sale. Even the most adept of marketing organizations knows there is a measurable fudge factor here.

Most of the traffic to our site is direct, meaning, people typing our domain name into a browser, clicking on a link that we can't track, or just typing our company name into a search box. But what leads to direct traffic?

We invest a fair bit of our budget in conferences. While we don't see much of an immediate measurable return (e.g., people coming to our trade show booth and writing their information down), we see an increase in direct traffic and conversion rates in the weeks that follow. In times where we were more critical of our investment and pulled back, we saw a slow decline. Related? We hope. We believe our conference appearances create a *halo effect* that increases our brands' perception in the market, which leads to definite yet indirect growth.

This applies to relationship marketing as well. A big part of our strategy is not just being at conferences and passively talking to anyone who wants to, but trying to generate as much *word of mouth* as possible. Usually this is in the form of onstage mentions. Thankfully, we are fortunate enough to have many of our early adopters and best customers grace the stage at many trade shows. Yes, we have a great product, but we also found that, as we invested more in building personal and authentic relationships with them, the number of onstage mentions went up. Did we go in specifically asking for that? No, we built a relationship, and *showed that we cared about who they were beyond just a credit card number we billed every month*. And while I am sure that they might have spoken about us anyway, we have the conviction that the relationship *helps*.

If people click on a listing of yours on a search portal, there may have been other prior touchpoints between you and them, and more touchpoints after the fact may contribute to a closed opportunity. They may have seen your ad online. Or they may have mutual contacts who shared they had a positive experience with you.

As with any type of marketing activity, one must seek answers in the leading indicators from your actions, the opportunities one can somewhat confidently associate with one's actions, and a fair bit of intuition.

Early in our history, we partnered with one of our customers to verify that their investment was worth it. Qualitatively, we had been hearing enough stories to give us confidence that the product was working, but there was a desire to get hard numbers around ROI. The solution was to combine usage data of Contactually with sales data for the whole brokerage. We were then able to see the sales trends of those who were using Contactually with those who weren't. Sure enough, the population of Contactually users saw a measured increase relative to the rest, to the order of 42 percent more sales! Thankfully, our team had enough humility to show that, while directionally we were very much worth it, there are other factors that played into that success. Did those who use Contactually become better because of us? Or were those professionals the ones who were looking to grow their business, and therefore, were using Contactually among many other activities?

We will never know with certainty. However, the goal of outcome tracking is to see, directionally, *is my business better with relationship marketing? Am I better?* If the answer is yes, then keep on going.

GETTING TACTICAL

How you implement it—the timing, tactics, and approaches—is for you to own and iterate. The point is to customize these to your needs.

Make the Ask

- Write down, as clearly as possible, what it is that you're seeking. Keep that top of mind for whenever you receive a prompt.

- Put that wherever you feel appropriate. E-mail signatures and social profiles are a good start.

- Determine what will work best for you to proactively solicit opportunities from your relationships. For some, it might be informing your sphere what would be valuable to you, should they come across the ideal opportunity. In other cases, it might be more direct.

Track Indicators

- Ensure that whatever you are using for engagement can track open, click, and reply rates.

- Note whenever one of your "untraceable" outreaches generates a response.

- Measure the response rates to your activities, and as you have the bandwidth, test different approaches, such as a different e-mail subject line.

- Track the health of your relationships relative to your goals, and review regularly. If possible, your database should give you a real-time score, which you can review daily.

When Receiving an Opportunity

- Say thank you!

- Mark the provider of the opportunity as far higher priority than those who have yet to provide an opportunity, which should in turn elicit a more elevated relationship approach.

- Record that as an outcome in your database, to allow you to measure what actions generate what results.

QUICK WIN

What if someone were to ask you, "What would be most valuable for you?" Prepare the answer to that question in a succinct one-liner, memorize it, and post that in your e-mail signature and social profiles.

KEY TAKEAWAYS

- Everyone will have a different approach to asking their network for opportunities, but a starting point is to ensure your sphere is educated on what would be helpful—and to be ready if asked.

- If and when an opportunity arrives, track where it came from and how it came, and remember that the people who have provided you with an opportunity are the ones most likely to do it again, so prioritize appropriately.

- Tracking the exact ROI of relationship marketing is challenging; however, one can track the leading indicators—such as open and reply rates—to gain a quick perspective of your attempts to deepen relationships.

CHAPTER

14

HOW IT WORKS IN THE REAL WORLD

Consider this chapter the CliffsNotes on the CAPITAL strategy. In fact, if this is the *first* chapter you're reading—just like the savages who read the ending of fiction novels first—the following pages may serve as a template for your own strategy.

At the risk of sounding like a broken record (to quote Plato, *"There is no harm in repeating a good thing"*), I will restate the fundamental basis of the CAPITAL strategy. The strategy and its actual execution is relatively straightforward and easy to understand. The beast to slay is the near-inability to act consistently over long time horizons, particularly when the reward may not present itself until a much later date.

Remember, dogmatic implementation of whatever I lay out for you may not be the best solution. It's up to you to adapt the strategy to how you work.

Note that I'm intentionally reassembling the CAPITAL strategy into a more chronological order. Bring on the bullet points!

SET YOUR GOALS

What do you seek from your sphere of influence? At the core, you need to identify what you seek to achieve.

231

- What are you looking to achieve in your business and career? Will relationships help you close more business? Will they help set you apart in a commoditized industry? Is the goal to retain more business? Do you just like to network, or build your brand?

- What would success look like, and how will you measure it? Are you looking to get more opportunities, increase your referrals, complete a specific task, gain more social capital?

ACT WITH CONSISTENCY

Acting with consistency is *the* biggest challenge you will encounter. Building habit is a key tool.

- If you are someone who is driven by your calendar, set a recurring calendar appointment.

- You may also set an alarm on your phone or computer to go off at a certain time every day.

- Associate this to something you already do, rather than trying to establish a new practice in isolation. Put a sticky note next to your computer monitor so it's the first thing you see when you sit down at your desk.

- After doing anything that nurtures your sphere, be sure to give yourself some kind of immediate reward.

- Remember that you *will* fall off the wagon.

AGGREGATE ALL OF YOUR RELATIONSHIPS INTO ONE PLACE

The foundation of nurturing your sphere of influence is having everything you need in one place.

- Pick a database. Even if it's as low-tech as a spreadsheet on your computer. Appendix A contains a list of possible solutions.

- Import all of your contacts there—professional, personal, old jobs, every social account. You want a digital copy of whatever has passed in and out of your brain.

- Whether assisted by artificial intelligence or done manually by you, clean up the database by merging duplicate contacts into a single record, and archive (*not permanently delete*) relationships you have high confidence have no personal or professional relevance.

- Set a monthly reminder to:
  - Re-upload a fresh export of whatever information sources your CRM does not automatically retrieve, as well as add any new data sources.
  - Manage any duplicate contacts.
  - For any recently added contacts, archive contacts that have no personal or professional relevance.

PRIORITIZE YOUR RELATIONSHIPS

Not everyone in your database is important. And some are more important than others.

- Based on the overall goals you've set for yourself, what types of relationships are most likely able to help you?

- Where can you find these people?

- Create categories or buckets in your database that reflect these groups of people.

- Set a cadence for each of the buckets. Start with the intention to follow up with each group of people every 90 days. If there is greater urgency to engage more frequently, adjust as appropriate (keep in mind that the more often you engage with a greater number of people, the more work you're committing to). If they are of low priority and urgency, consider engaging only once or twice a year.

- Prioritize the people in your database into the structure you've created. Set reasonable goals for yourself; 10 people in your highest-priority categories, 20 people the next level down, 100 in the lowest, etc.

- On an ongoing basis:
  - As you are interacting with new people, prioritize them on the fly, especially if your database has tools to easily support that.
  - If there's been a major change of status (e.g., you complete a project with someone), update their priority.

- Set a weekly reminder to:
  - Prioritize relationships that you've interacted with recently.

- Monthly:
  - Revisit the buckets that you have and reprioritize the relationships.

- Quarterly:
  - Repeat the first three steps to see if there's a change you need to make in your prioritization based on the current state of your business or any evolution in strategy. Make any changes as necessary. Don't be afraid to start fresh!

GATHER INTELLIGENCE

Know more about the people you want to know you.

- Ensure your intelligent database is set up to automatically augment each contact with information it may have access to.

- Follow your contacts on appropriate social platforms, keeping in mind that personal feeds are acceptable as long as they are publicly available and/or you already have some relationship with them.

- Subscribe to a service that notifies you of news or major updates that may be relevant to them.

- During every interaction:
  - Take copious notes.
  - Engage in small talk and capture seemingly unimportant and irrelevant information (recent or future trips, kids' names, past or upcoming life events).
  - Enter all this into your database, as well as the time and location of the interaction.
  - Set reminders for any specific upcoming events, and recurring reminders for birthdays, personal and professional anniversaries, or any discrete follow-up items.

- When doing research:
  - Review past interactions for relevant hooks: personal information, travel, open actions.
  - Do your web research using both personal and professional sources.
  - Research their company, their industry, and any of their main interests for recent news.
  - Capture any bits of information you've uncovered in your database for future use.

ENGAGE AND ADD VALUE

Staying top of mind is not just about following up; it's about demonstrating that you are a trusted, valuable, and personal relationship that deserves to be maintained.

- Identify how much resources and effort you want to invest in your contacts relative to your own availability, their importance, and the number of people of similar or higher priority.

- Review your previously gathered intelligence, as well as do additional research to see what recent updates might yield relevant information or needs.

- Know there is no right or wrong approach, as long as your interaction is personal, relevant, and valuable to them.

- If there's a specific challenge or personal priority you've identified, attempt to solve that.

- Be profuse in your gratitude for any past good deed they've done for you and demonstrate your ROI from it.

- Buy a gift that's relevant to them, not one that markets you.

- Lend your own social capital and make double opt-in introductions that could aid them.

- Create communal social objects through meals or other events by carefully curating the memorable experiences for a carefully chosen group of people.

- Don't be afraid to send a prewritten e-mail with a general check-in, a text message sharing that you're thinking of them, or something else that takes very little effort. Don't give them extra work. Just demonstrate that you care about them and are thinking about them.

- Annually or quarterly:
  - Build a set of e-mail templates that you can reuse.
  - Identify a number of gifts (books, etc.) that you can easily pick and send out.
  - Buy stationery and stamps for handwritten cards.

SEAN CARPENTER, REAL ESTATE TRAINER AND SPEAKER

If you want to go running in the morning, if you wake up and the first thing you see is your running shoes right by your bed, that's your trigger to put them on. If you put them on, you're more likely to get out the door and go for a walk or a run. I try to be as disciplined and as consistent as possible. I try to get to the office each morning and do what I call my 4H Club, which takes me about 45 minutes. Just like seeing my running shoes by the bed, I have a note attached to my office monitor that tells me it's time for the 4H Club. The 4H Club is really simple. It's a way to make sure that if I do nothing else the rest of the day, I've done something to build relationships. Afterward, I'm intentional about rewarding myself; I go get my iced coffee.

The first H is I write five *Handwritten notes*. Those go to people in my sphere of influence, to anyone I need to thank for something, or to the next person on my contact list I haven't talked to in a while. There's no special reason behind doing five versus four or six. Five works for me. It's not too many. What matters is that I'm doing more than one of each activity.

Now sometimes, if I don't really have anything to say that warrants a handwritten note, I'll send a report on their local housing market and write a quick note on it. It just says, "Hey, it's me. I hope things are going well. Reach out with any questions." Hand addressing everything also makes it clear this is coming from me, not part of a mass mailing.

The second H is my *Hot sheet*. I run the hot sheet for my local real estate market to see what new listings there may be, price changes, or anything like that. I say to myself, "Is there anyone I know who lives within a two- or three-block radius of that property?" If there is, I call, text, or e-mail them that listing.

The third H is *Happy birthdays*. I go on Facebook and I see which of my friends are having birthdays. I send them a message—a little more than just a happy birthday message. It's about a couple of paragraphs of wishes. It stands out from all the other ones. If it's someone who I have a closer relationship with, I'll send a video text message to wish them a happy birthday.

The last H is what I call my *High fives*. I'm socially driven. I try to build relationships on social media channels as well. I'll do five likes and five comments on Facebook. Then I'll jump over to Twitter, and I'll do five retweets or five comments or five engagements. I do the same thing on Instagram. I'll send five random texts to someone on my phone, "Have a great day," "Hope things are going well," "Let's get together." Just a text. Sometimes those are video texts, and sometimes they're typed out.

GET AND TRACK RESULTS

As much as you believe in possessing a giving mentality, this isn't pure charity.

- Don't be afraid to make the ask. You're soliciting people you care about and genuinely want to help.

- Make it clear—on your website and social profiles, e-mail footers and periodic messages—what would be a valuable opportunity or introduction you'd appreciate.

- Track your outcomes, as well as open rates, response rates, and other metrics of your sphere of influence.

CONCLUSION

We made it!

I hope this is the beginning of a new chapter in your personal and professional journey.

I've experienced and been witness to truly amazing outcomes from knowing the right people at the right time. I can say my life wouldn't be what it is today were it not for knowing the right people—and the right people knowing me. That's been helped by plenty of luck and timing, for which I'm thankful.

I will close with one point that I haven't dwelled on too much in this book so far.

You're going to screw up.

And that is *awesome*.

Someone you meant to engage with will slip through the cracks, and you will miss out on amazing opportunities because of it. I blew it, you'll say.

You'll be told by others not to message them again. I've burned that bridge, you'll say.

Many of your outreaches will be incredibly embarrassing. What was I thinking, you'll say.

You'll host a dinner, and it'll seem like a near-total failure. This is impossible, you'll say.

You'll buy a gift, and the recipient won't acknowledge it. That was a waste, you'll say.

I have erred *countless* times when it comes to my sphere—and I still do, every day.

I've forgotten people that I *still* kick myself for today. I've embarrassed myself with weak introductions. I've harassed people into a phone call or coffee meeting, only to have nothing to say. I haven't done my research and sounded like a complete ignoramus.

The truth is *everyone* is guilty of this. Many of the experts who contributed to this book and the thinking behind it noted how they had erred.

When I say it's awesome that you make these mistakes, I mean that I want you to treat these failures as amazing learning opportunities. Failure is a core part of our lives. What separates the wheat from the chaff, the great from the good, is the ability to let failure be a lesson. So just take another step forward. It's not the end of the road.

Onward and upward!

ACKNOWLEDGMENTS

I am incredibly thankful that I get to wake up and follow my passions (well, most days) at Contactually, and this book is a product of that. Both also would have no chance of existing in their current forms were it not for many others. Thousands of people made contributions to this book—from the many people we've employed at Contactually over the years, the dozens of mentors and advisors who have helped shape our thinking, to the tens of thousands of customers who validate what we do.

We were fortunate to have a beginner's mindset early on, and we were sponges to the ideas shared with us by many experts in the field of relationship marketing. One person stands head and shoulders above others, and has since the early days: Patrick Ewers. Patrick was the first one to really take a bet on us, and he elevated our theoretical approach with his years of experience serving as relationship coach to top venture capitalists and captains of industry.

To the tens of thousands of users we've had over the years at Contactually, watching what you responded to, what worked and what didn't, what you liked and didn't like, was the best guidance and proving ground for our CAPITAL strategy. Your stories of how working with us dramatically impacted your lives, your businesses, and your relationships for the better kept us going through the dark times.

To the team at Contactually, I could write an entire book of acknowledgments for what you've done to take that initial idea to the heights we've achieved over the past eight years. When the idea for a book first came up in 2015, you were nothing but supportive, reviewing outlines, titles, drafts, and marketing plans. Whatever you could do, you helped. This includes Audie and Deidre at Lion & Orb and our board, especially Don Rainey, who always encouraged that we share our thought leadership with the world.

My two research interns, Tanner Hackney and Elizabeth Jaye, really helped elevate a book of best practices with the deep research that you see throughout here.

So many successful authors I look up to made their calendars and experiences available to someone who hadn't earned it: Dorie Clark, Derek Coburn, Jayson Gaignard, John Ruhlin, Tucker Max, Susan RoAne, Michelle Lederman, Ian Altman, and others I'm surely forgetting. Joey Coleman, not only did you share your playbook with me, but you introduced me to Sara, whose impact on my writing has been immeasurable.

Our publishing team, led by Sara Stibitz, invested countless hours to help refine my patchwork quilt of thoughts and best practices into a cohesive narrative and proposal. I am forever thankful for you taking a chance on me and introducing me to Jim Levine, our book agent. Jim (and Matthew), you've worked with such amazing talent, I'm still not sure what I'm doing among them.

My editor, Casey Ebro, and her team at McGraw-Hill, thank you for taking a bet on a first-time author. I nearly fainted when I saw the number of pencil marks on the first draft, but with your guidance, I realized how every word needs to belong.

My cofounders at Contactually, Tony and Jeff, you took a bet, quit your jobs, moved across the country, and started a company with me on nothing much more than an idea jotted down in Evernote. I'll never forget that.

Catherine Butler, you helped unlock my love of writing in elementary school, something I will carry with me for the rest of my life. There's no way a fourth grader writing short stories about his teacher getting blown up and eaten by dragons would be received well these days, but you encouraged me to just keep writing.

Finally, thanks to all my friends and family who believed in me and let me disappear on weekends to work on this. Alex and D, I owe you a few dozen manuscript-writing-free beach days.

APPENDICES

For **updates on these** resources visit the digital appendix at http://successisinyoursphere.com/appendix.

APPENDIX A: TOOLS

CRM Database Platforms

The CAPITAL strategy relies on having a central source of record for all your relationships and relationship intelligence. The best CRM is the one *you* use, so find the right platform that serves your needs.

- Contactually
- FullContact
- Google Contacts
- Cloze
- Nimble
- Salesforce

- Google Sheets
- Top Producer
- Airtable
- Nudge
- Affinity
- Streak

Helpful Technology Tools

These tools aid your relationship marketing strategy by either helping you act more efficiently or giving you skills not otherwise available.

- TextExpander
- Grammarly
- Evercontact

- Nuzzle
- Slydial
- BombBomb

APPENDIX B: SAMPLE BUCKETS

Consultant

Bucket Name	Reminder Interval
Active Clients	30 days
Past Clients A	90 days
Past Clients B	180 days
Prospective Clients	90 days
Active Opportunities	14 days
Referral Sources	90 days

Real Estate Agent

Bucket Name	Reminder Interval
Active Clients	14 days
Past Clients A	60 days
Past Clients B	365 days
Top Referrers	30 days
Cold Leads	180 days
Warm Leads	60 days
Sphere of Influence	30 days
Internet Leads	5 days

Business Owner

Bucket Name	Reminder Interval
Current Customers	30 days
Past Customers	90 days
Advisors/Mentors	45 days
Investors	60 days
Referral Partners	60 days
Potential Customers	90 days
Potential Hires	90 days

Mortgage Broker

Bucket Name	Reminder Interval
Past Clients	90 days
Active Leads	60 days
Current Clients	30 days
Referral Partners	60 days
Professional Colleagues	120 days

Venture Capital

Bucket Name	Reminder Interval
Entrepreneurs	90 days
LPs	45 days
VCs	120 days
Portfolio CEOs	60 days
Prospective CEOs	120 days
Prospective LPs	45 days
Professional Colleagues	120 days

APPENDIX C: MESSAGE TEMPLATES

Quick Ping

Subject: Just thought of you

Hey {{ first_name | fallback: "there" }},

Saw something just now and thought of you. Realized we haven't had a chance to connect.

No need to respond if you're busy—just wanted to say hi. Hope you're well!

Just Touching Base

Subject: Hi {{ first_name | fallback: "there" }}, just touching base

---

Hey {{ first_name | fallback: "there" }},

I know we haven't spoken in a while, so I just wanted to touch base. As always, I'm here as a resource for you, so just let me know if you have any questions about new features, best practices, or anything in between!

As soon as you run into a question or concern, please let me know by e-mail or you can call {{ phone_number | fallback: ""}}.

If you're having a great experience with {{ company | fallback: "your company" }} so far, would you be interested in referring us to your network?

Kindly,

Nice Meeting You

Subject: Truly a pleasure meeting you

Hi {{ first_name | fallback: "there" }},

I just wanted you to know that I genuinely enjoyed getting to meet you, albeit briefly. Instead of just sending you information on me, I'd love to know more about you! I value each of my new relationships highly, and don't want to send you "blanket" information.

So tell me—what's been going well for you and your business lately? What challenges are you encountering? I'm happy to assist in any way possible, even if it means connecting you to someone else I know who may be a better fit.

Looking forward to connecting more in-depth.

Cheers,

Post–Networking Event

Subject: Just following up!

Hello {{ first_name | fallback: "there" }},

It was great getting a chance to meet you! I was wondering if you wanted to find a time for us to continue our conversation about [INSERT TOPIC]. If you're interested, just send me some times that work for you, I'm sure we can find a time that accommodates both of our busy schedules.

I'm looking forward to chatting soon,

Introduction

> Subject: Brief Introduction—{{ contact_2_first_name }} meet {{ contact_1_first_name }}
>
> Hi {{ contact_1_first_name | fallback: "there" }},
>
> I was speaking with {{ contact_2_first_name }} recently, and I learned that {{ contact_2_first_name}} is {{ contact_2_intro_summary}}.
>
> Hi {{ contact_2_first_name | fallback: "there" }},
>
> {{ contact_1_first_name | fallback: "" }} is a connection/colleague/friend/good friend of mine who is {{ contact_1_intro_summary | fallback: "" }}.
>
> I hope you two can connect with each other to keep the conversation going. Please let me know if I can help in any other way.
>
> Best,

Scheduling a Call

> Subject: Let's schedule a call
>
> Hi {{ first_name | fallback: "there" }},
>
> I hope you're doing well. I was hoping we could hop on the phone soon to get a better idea of what you're interested in and what I can do to help.
>
> Are you available on Monday between INSERT TIME? Please let me know if there's a more convenient time. Also, is {{ contact_phone_number | fallback: "" }} still your preferred number?
>
> Looking forward to connecting soon,

Sharing an Article

Subject: I think you'll appreciate this {{ first_name | fallback: "" }}

Hey {{ first_name | fallback: "there" }},

I came across this article {{INSERT ARTICLE LINK}}. Saw it and thought of you.

I'd love to hear your feedback on the subject and maybe we can get together sometime soon to discuss it.

Hope everything is going well!

Cheers,

Asking for a Testimonial

Subject: Quick Request

Hey {{ first_name | fallback: "there" }},

Do you have five minutes? I'm reaching out to you with a quick request.

I've found that more people are looking online or on social media to find reviews before they even consider buying. I'm not just looking to be propped up with positive reviews—I'd love if you could give your genuine feedback on your experience with me, in the hopes that future clients will find your insight valuable.

I'd be grateful if you'd submit a review on {{Website}}!

Thank you!

Thank You for a Review

Subject: Thank You for Your {{Website}} Endorsement

Hi {{ first_name | fallback: "there" }},

Thank you for your endorsement on {{Website}}. As a person who gives professional advice to other people, I rely on what my peers, customers, and partners are saying about me and the value I bring to each of you.

I appreciate the fact that you took the time to make that investment in me. Please let me know if there is something I can do for you in return.

All the best,

One-Year Anniversary (Ideal for Real Estate, but Easily Tweaked for Other Applications)

Subject: Happy One Year in Your Home!

Hi {{ first_name | fallback: "there" }},

Happy anniversary on the purchase of your home! I imagine you've settled in nicely at your place now. However, if there is anything I can help with, please don't hesitate to ask.

Also, as you know, real estate is strongly based on relationships. If you know of anyone who is searching for a Realtor, I'd be honored to have you pass along my information, or reply with their name and contact info.

Hope to hear from you soon and thank you so much!

Best,

APPENDIX D: READING LIST

* *

Book Yourself Solid: The Fastest, Easiest, and Most Reliable System for Getting More Clients Than You Can Handle Even if You Hate Marketing and Selling by Michael Port, 2008

Croissants vs. Bagels: Strategic, Effective, and Inclusive Networking at Conferences by Robbie Samuels, 2017

The 11 Laws of Likability: Relationship Networking . . . Because People Do Business with People They Like by Michelle Lederman, 2011

Friend of a Friend: Understanding the Hidden Networks That Can Transform Your Life and Your Career by David Burkus, 2018

Giftology: The Art and Science of Using Gifts to Cut Through the Noise, Increase Referrals, and Strengthen Client Retention by John Ruhlin, 2016

Give and Take: Why Helping Others Drives Our Success by Adam Grant, 2013

The Go-Giver, Expanded Edition: A Little Story About a Powerful Business Idea by Bob Burg and John David Mann

Hooked: How to Build Habit-Forming Products by Nir Eyal and Ryan Hoover, 2014

How to Win Friends and Influence People by Dale Carnegie, 1937

How to Work a Room: The Ultimate Guide to Making Lasting Connections by Susan RoAne, 1988

Mastermind Dinners: Build Lifelong Relationships by Connecting Experts, Influencers, and Linchpins by Jayson Gaignard, 2014

Networking Is Not Working: Stop Collecting Business Cards and Start Making Meaningful Connections by Derek Coburn, 2014

Never Eat Alone by Keith Ferrazzi, 2005

Ninja Selling: Subtle Skills. Big Results. by Larry Kendall, 2017

Stand Out by Dorie Clark, 2015

Superconnector: Stop Networking and Start Building Business Relationships That Matter by Scott Gerber and Ryan Paugh, 2018

Top of Mind: Use Content to Unleash Your Influence and Engage Those Who Matter to You by John Hall, 2017

NOTES

CHAPTER 1

1. Morton Deutsch and Harold B. Gerard. "A Study of Normative and Informational Social Influences upon Individual Judgment," *The Journal of Abnormal and Social Psychology* 51, no. 3 (1955): 629–36, doi:10.1037/h0046408; Robert Schnuerch and Henning Gibbons, "Social Proof in the Human Brain: Electrophysiological Signatures of Agreement and Disagreement with the Majority," *Psychophysiology* 52, no. 10 (2015): 1328–342, doi:10.1111/psyp.12461.
2. Jacques Launay and Robin I. M. Dunbar, "Playing with Strangers: Which Shared Traits Attract Us Most to New People?" *PLOS ONE* 10, no. 6 (2015): 1, doi:10.1371/journal.pone.0129688.
3. M. R. Welch, D. Sikkink, and M. T. Loveland, "The Radius of Trust: Religion, Social Embeddedness and Trust in Strangers," *Social Forces* 86, no. 1 (2007): 25, doi:10.1353/sof.2007.0116.
4. M. R. Welch, D. Sikkink, and M. T. Loveland, "The Radius of Trust: Religion, Social Embeddedness and Trust in Strangers"; Jacques Launay and Robin I. M. Dunbar, "Playing with Strangers: Which Shared Traits Attract Us Most to New People?"
5. James S. Coleman, "Social Capital in the Creation of Human Capital," *American Journal of Sociology* 94 (1988): 95–120; Brian Keeley, "6. A Bigger Picture," Human Capital (OECD Insights, 2007), 102–5.
6. National Association of Realtors, 2016 Member Safety Report, November 2, 2016, https://www.nar.realtor/reports/2016-member-safety-report.
7. "The Fire," *The Office*, Season 2, Episode 4, ABC, October 11, 2005.
8. Frederick F. Reichheld and Thomas Teal, *The Loyalty Effect: The Hidden Force Behind Growth, Profits, and Lasting Value* (Boston, MA: Harvard Business School Press, 2008).
9. Phillip E. Pfeifer, "The Optimal Ratio of Acquisition and Retention Costs," *Journal of Targeting, Measurement and Analysis for Marketing* 13, no. 2 (2005), doi:10.1057/palgrave.jt.5740142; Fred Reichheld, "Prescription for Cutting Costs," Bain & Company, 2001; Philipp Schmitt, Bernd Skiera, and Christophe Van Den Bulte, "Referral Programs and Customer Value," *Journal of Marketing* 75, no. 1 (2011), doi:10.1509/jmkg.75.1.46.

CHAPTER 2

1. Maria Konnikova, "The Limits of Friendship," *The New Yorker*, October 7, 2014.
2. R. A. Hill and R. I. M. Dunbar, "Social Network Size in Humans," *Human Nature* 14, no. 1 (2003).
3. R. Dunbar, "Evolution of the Social Brain," *Science* 302, no. 5648 (2003).
4. Larry Squire, "Is Photographic Memory Real? If So, How Does It Work?" BrainFacts.org, April 17, 2013, http://www.brainfacts.org /Ask-an-Expert/Is-photographic-memory-real.
5. Sophie Portrat, Pierre Barrouillet, and Valérie Camos, "Time-Related Decay or Interference-Based Forgetting in Working Memory?" *Journal of Experimental Psychology: Learning, Memory, and Cognition* 34, no. 6 (2008), doi:10.1037/a0013356.
6. "Secrets of a Successful Marriage," *The Simpsons*, FOX, Season 5, Episode 22, May 19, 1994.
7. Klaus Oberauer and Stephan Lewandowsky, "Forgetting in Immediate Serial Recall: Decay, Temporal Distinctiveness, or Interference?" *Psychological Review* 115, no. 3 (2008): , doi:10.1037/0033-295x.115.3.544.
8. Johanna Lass-Hennemann et al., "Stress Strengthens Memory of First Impressions of Others' Positive Personality Traits," *PLOS ONE* 6, no. 1 (January 26, 2011), doi:10.1371/journal.pone.0016389.
9. Johanna Lass-Hennemann et al., "Stress Strengthens Memory of First Impressions of Others' Positive Personality Traits."
10. Cornelia Wrzus et al., "Social Network Changes and Life Events Across the Life Span: A Meta-analysis," *Psychological Bulletin* 139, no. 1 (2013), doi:10.1037/a0028601.
11. S. M. McClure et al., "Separate Neural Systems Value Immediate and Delayed Monetary Rewards," *Science* 306, no. 5695 (2004), doi:10.1126/science.1100907.
12. Mark Murphy, "Interruptions at Work Are Killing Your Productivity," *Forbes*, October 3, 2016, https://www.forbes.com/sites /markmurphy/2016/10/30/interruptions-at-work-are-killing-your -productivity/#3466eab81689.

CHAPTER 3

1. https://www.nar.realtor/sites/default/files/migration_files /Highlights-NAR-HBS-2013.pdf.

CHAPTER 4

1. If you're not a sci-fi movie buff, the protagonist dons a large robotic suit that gives her superhuman strength, allowing her to take on a very irate creature.

CHAPTER 5

1. An excellent resource here is *When* by Daniel Pink if you are interested in exploring further.
2. http://tinyhabits.com/.
3. https://www.psychologistworld.com/memory/zeigarnik-effect-interruptions-memory.
4. Michael Chaiton et al., "Estimating the Number of Quit Attempts It Takes to Quit Smoking Successfully in a Longitudinal Cohort of Smokers," *BMJ Open*, 2016: 1–9.

CHAPTER 6

1. Yes, some geek out there just read that phrase and is pining over the good ol' days of Mashable, TechCrunch, and Twitter.

CHAPTER 8

1. Hugh MacLeod, "Social Objects: Everything You Ever Wanted to Know!" Gapingvoid, December 31, 2007, https://www.gapingvoid.com/blog/2007/12/31/social-objects-for-beginners/.
2. First Round Review, "A Venture Capitalist Explains How to Become Insanely Well-Connected," Quartz, April 25, 2017, https://qz.com/968424/first-round-capitals-chris-fralic-a-venture-capitalist-explains-how-to-become-insanely-well-connected-and-networked/.
3. Janice Nadler, "Rapport in Legal Negotiation: How Small Talk Can Facilitate E-Mail Dealmaking," *Harvard Negotiation Law Review* 9, no. 223 (2004): 223–50.

CHAPTER 9

1. R. A. Emmons and M. E. McCullough, "Counting Blessings Versus Burdens: An Experimental Investigation of Gratitude and Subjective Well-Being in Daily Life," *Journal of Personality and Social Psychology* 84, no. 2 (2003): 377–89.

CHAPTER 10

1. As proof, our editor commented on this line: "You did that with me! And I liked that. It made me feel as if you were paying attention to what I was doing but sort of staying above the fray."

CHAPTER 11

1. If for nothing else than to add the line "and if you decide you don't like them—you're a mile away from them and they don't have shoes!" Dad jokes.

2. Thank you, Jayson Gaignard, for this one. His exact wording is, "If we were to buy a bottle of champagne a year from now to celebrate, what are we celebrating?" Ready for that bottle when you are, my friend.

3. Michael I. Norton, Daniel Mochon, and Dan Ariely, The "IKEA Effect": When Labor Leads to Love," Working Paper 11-091, 2011, http://www.hbs.edu/faculty/Publication%20Files/11-091.pdf.

CHAPTER 12

1. One of the earlier and most notable cases was back in 2012, when the retailer Target identified a series of product purchases that predicted that someone was pregnant. They sent diaper coupons to the home of a teenage girl, before her parents knew she was pregnant. Drama ensued, of course. https://digit.hbs.org/submission/target-using-predictive-analytics-to-increase-value-capture/.

CHAPTER 13

1. https://en.wikipedia.org/wiki/Reality_distortion_field.

2. https://mailchimp.com/resources/research/email-marketing-benchmarks/.

INDEX

ABOUT THE AUTHOR

Zvi Band is the cofounder and CEO of Contactually, an intelligent CRM platform for relationship-oriented businesses. Without manual data entry, Contactually automatically tracks every e-mail conversation, meeting, phone call, and text message and leverages its immense data set and predictive analytics to identify proactively which key relationships are due for engagement and then assists the user in making the best outreach possible. Contactually's functionality has resulted in a measured increase in the gross income of clients using the platform.

Zvi is an active speaker, writer, and podcaster on the topic of relationship marketing. Zvi is regularly interviewed for articles and podcasts, and he has been listed in Forbes's 25 Professional Networking Experts to Watch.

A prominent promoter of entrepreneurship and technology businesses in the greater Washington, DC, region, Zvi founded Proudly Made In DC, a site marketing the start-ups in DC and serving as a starting point for entrepreneurs. He is also the cofounder and coorganizer of the DC Tech Meetup, which has grown to be one of the largest meetups in the country with over 20,000 members and 700+ in attendance at monthly meetings. Zvi has created DC Tech Summer, where 550+ interns apply to work at 20 start-ups every summer. He is advisor to a number of companies and is a proud mentor to Acceleprise, an enterprise technology accelerator.

A finalist for Ernst and Young's 2016 Entrepreneur of the Year award, Zvi has been listed as one of DC's Top 40 fastest-growing CEOs, 50 on Fire, and for six years running as one of *Washingtonian* magazine's Tech Titans. He has been ranked on Swanepoel's Most Powerful People in The Residential Real Estate Brokerage Industry, REAL Trend's 2019 Game Changers, and HousingWire's Tech 100.

Zvi lives outside of Washington, DC, with his wife and family—including an obnoxious cocker spaniel.